5,378 Tips for a BETTER LIFE,

Hotter *Sex*, Fresher Breath, Thicker Hair,

Thinner THIGHS and Cleaner Laundry!

(not necessarily in that order)

ALSO BY LINDA CULLEN

Double Exposure – The book (with Bob Robertson)

5,378 Tips for a BETTER LIFE, Hotter *Sex*, Fresher Breath, Thicker Hair, Thinner THIGHS and Cleaner Laundry!

(not necessarily in that order)

by

Linda Cullen

iUniverse, Inc.

New York   Bloomington

5,378 Tips for a Better Life, Hotter Sex, Fresher Breath, Thicker Hair, Thinner Thighs and Cleaner Laundry! (not necessarily in that order)

iUniverse books may be ordered through booksellers or by contacting:

iUniverse
1663 Liberty Drive
Bloomington, IN 47403
www.iuniverse.com
1-800-Authors (1-800-288-4677)

ISBN: 978-1-4401-2342-9 (pbk)
ISBN: 978-1-4401-2343-6 (ebk)

Library of Congress Control Number: 2009925373

Printed in the United States of America

iUniverse rev. date:3/30/2009

Cover photo by Tim Matheson

THANKS

To Mom & Dad for passing on some recessive genes which have come in handy

To my editor at 24 Hours, Dean Broughton, for taking a chance on me

And most especially, to Bob, for always saying "YES" to coffee and muffins. KBO

Contents

Introduction

I know what you're saying. "Why? Why put a book of funny columns like this together now?" Well, I did it because in these troubled times, I felt that what people really need is something to lift their spirits and give them a respite from their fears, their worries, their jobs filled with drudgery, in the hope that some kind of happiness may spread from one person to another which might then lead to WORLD PEACE!...plus I had some spare time. The truth is I have been writing my column for Vancouver's 24 Hours for almost 5 years and the response has been so positive that I realized some folks might actually like to read some of these columns again, and possibly buy hundreds and hundreds of copies for their friends and family so that they may also get in on the fun, and perhaps lead to that WORLD PEACE thing again, but, that's not mandatory...really...no pressure. I've been writing and performing comedy for, gee, over 20 years now, and the only thing I really want from it is laughter. So, please enjoy 5,378 Tips etc., and if by some fluke, it does lead to world peace, well, there's no need to thank me...really...truly...okay, if you insist.

5,378 Tips for a Better Life...
blah, blah, blah

Here's a Tip

This week I'm running the first excerpt from my self-help book *5,378 tips for a Better Life, Hotter Sex, Fresher Breath, Thicker Hair, Thinner Thighs and Cleaner Laundry! (not necessarily in that order)* The book isn't available in stores yet. Well, to be honest, it isn't even written yet, however I think this will be a great beginning.* Every one of these tips has been test driven by me, and are guaranteed to change your life in a profound way, or at least take your mind off the mother of all recessions for a while.

TIP #1: TAKE DOWN THE ICICLES – you know who you are. You've had those Christmas icicle lights hanging on your house for somewhere between 2 and 10 years. Come on! Do you really think you're fooling us?

"Honey, look at that house. It's June and it has icicles hanging from the eaves."

"Yeh, and it's 28 degrees Celsius. We better phone the weather office and let them know! This could be a sign of Armageddon… or worse, a Bay City Rollers comeback! "

So take the icicles down. You'll feel better. And the good news is, it's only 6 months to Christmas.

TIP #2: If you are 15 seconds older than 40, STOP using the word "Cool" (pronounced Kee-oo-wall) if you are not discussing the weather. If you're using "Cool" in the company of teenagers in the hope that they will then think you actually are "Kee-oo-all", scientists have proven the exact opposite to be true. They developed an equation called The Celine Dion Conundrum: Gucci + Prada + Dior = Goofy Nerd in Gucci, Prada and Dior. Go figure.

TIP #3: DON'T buy any magazines that have Jessica Simpson, Ashley Simpson, Bart Simpson, OJ Simpson, Ashford and Simpson, the Olsen Twins, The Blues Brothers or anyone named Al on the cover. Because if you do, then Jessica, Ashley et Al will think that you actually care about them, or, heaven forbid, that you think they are "Kee-oo-wall."

TIP #4: If you ever actually meet a witch and then marry her, just like in the movie Bewitched, don't force her to hide her gifts, lecturing her with "We have to live regular lives, we mustn't have an unfair advantage over other normal folks." On the contrary, you must take that witch directly to the lottery kiosk, and then you must let her wiggle that nose and use her talents to their fullest while picking Super 7 numbers. By the way, if you do follow this tip, remember, when you collect your jackpot, you can send my large portion of the winnings care of this paper.

So, there are 5,374 tips to go, but right now the wind is getting up and the icicles are banging on the gutters. I better get them down.

*Well, looky here, I put the donuts down and finally go to work!

More Tips

You may have read *The Secret* and *The 7 Habits* but they pale in comparison to the *5,378 Tips* mainly because they are short by over 5 THOUSAND tips. Read carefully, because there will be a test when you finish all the tips…7 or 8 years from now.

TIP #36 – Never Go to a Party at Maya Angelou's House.

You know Maya. Oprah's mentor? She has a rule that if she hears anyone gossiping when she has a party, she throws them out! I can tell you the only reason I go to parties is to hear some gossip, speak some gossip, or behave in such a manner as to inspire some gossip. Here's a Maya party:

LINDA: Say Maya, did you hear about Charlene?

MAYA: Charlene is a wonderful person.

LINDA: What? Oh, yes…right…Charlene IS a wonderful person.

MAYA: So kind.

LINDA: Yes, kind….Hmmm…well…um…nice carrot sticks.

MAYA: Charlene made them.

LINDA: And she can make carrot sticks! Is there NOTHING Charlene can't do?

A normal party:

LINDA: Say, Kathy, did you hear about Charlene?

KATHY: That she's having a torrid affair with her plumber?

LINDA: Yes! Geez, there's nothing to eat except carrot sticks.

KATHY: Charlene made them.

LINDA: Well, who has time to *cook* when you're constantly getting your 'sump' pumped…if you know what I mean? Ha Ha! What a great party!

The secret to a long life is having fun. You won't live long if you go to a Maya soiree.

TIP #122—Don't Wear Shorts AND Socks

There are some men out there, you probably know one yourself, who wear shorts in the summer, but then also wear knee high socks so the only part of the leg that actually gets any air is the knee cap. This leads to a strange mutation of the well known "Farmer's Tan", called "The Nerd's Knees". The secret to success is making good choices. So choose the shorts. Ditch the socks. Otherwise you'll be the topic of discussion at one of the parties in Tip #36. And I think you know which party.

Tip #249 – Everything I Need To Know I Learned From Soap Operas

(This is a sub-set of rules that will give you a strong moral compass to follow in any situation)

-GIVEN THE OPPORTUNITY TO TELL THE TRUTH… DON'T! Keep secrets, tell lies and ALWAYS wear push up bras. Eg:

HUBBY: Say Charlene honey, I heard at a party that you've been getting your pipes unplugged by Gary the plumb…hey, is that a new push up bra?!..Um, what was I saying?

-FAKE AMNESIA. This takes a bit of acting, but, only a bit, I mean, you've seen the soaps.

CHARLENE: Darling, I banged my head! I can't remember if I'm having an affair"

HUBBY: Well, what did you bang your head on, sweetie?

CHARLENE: A tool belt!

That's it for this excerpt. Your life's getting better already.

The Answer Lady

I regularly get e-mails from readers who are quite frequently awake, and who request that I use my vast knowledge to educate the population or settle debates between parties. I'm happy to do this because I think a knowledgeable readership is a happier one, and it also burns up a few hours in my court appointed community service.

For example several weeks ago a Mr. Richard Richardson (or for short, Dick Dickson) wrote asking me to answer this question: Which has more charisma; Stephen Harper* or a B.C. Ferries scone? Well Dick, I think the answer is obvious. But I did the research anyway.

As it happens, both prime minister Harper and the scone were tested at the top secret Personality Accelerator at UBC and results showed that the scone was 46% more charismatic than Harper, but 12% less tasty. However, when the BC Ferries scone and Mr. Harper were both fired through a canon at a building, the prime minister caused 12% more damage than the scone. Something to be proud of.

Another conscious reader wrote asking me which way to go to avoid all the road construction in Vancouver.** Having been born and raised in this city, I know exactly how to avoid delays: go to Roberts Bank, get on a coal freighter and sail to Korea.

Finally, John Bysack wrote asking me to pontificate on divorce and included a few Sub-heading suggestions such as "Divorce Anniversary Get Togethers" and "Divorce Re-enactments". Quite frankly, these two ideas will only lead to the destruction of hundreds of sets of heirloom china, so my advice is, forget them.

Divorce is a Latin word meaning "What's yours is mine and what's mine is mine!" The first divorce took place in prehistoric times, when a Cro-Magnon wife, catching sight of the first Neanderthal, was swept away by his upright walking and substantially less body hair and so filed for divorce. The court transcripts went like this:

JUDGE: Mr. Magnon, what is the total value of your estate?

MAGNON: Me have ROCK!

JUDGE: Right, 50% of the rock to Mrs. Magnon.

MAGNON: Aargh! Me only half rock LEFT!

LAWYER: Not so fast Mr. Magnon. I'll take half of THAT!

MAGNON: Big AAARGH!

Coincidentally, that was also when the first lawyer was thrown into a volcano. Many famous people have been divorced: Taylor and Burton, Martin and Lewis, Cagney and Lacey, Sears and Roebuck. Most recently Reese Witherspoon and Ryan Phillipe have begun divorce proceedings after suddenly realizing that they're both only 12 years old.***

The important question today is; why are there so many divorces? Scientists have just discovered that divorce is caused by a virus that you can catch from a toilet seat…if it's left in the UPRIGHT position! Keep those cards and letters coming.

*Canada's current prime minister. A man who makes paint drying seem like an amusement park ride.

**Because we're getting the Olympics, and apparently they want to hold the Grande Slalom down all our main thoroughfares.

***Of course that's not true. They're really 14 years old. Their kids are 12.

Capital Offenses

Several weeks ago I had an outraged e-mail from an outraged *24 Hours* reader who was shocked, outraged, stunned, outraged, shaken NOT stirred and outraged by my frequent use of CAPITAL LETTERS in my columns. He suggested that *24 Hours* readers were intelligent enough to interpret the finer nuances of my intricately constructed humour without me resorting to cheap devises to hammer home my SUBTLE PUNCHLINES. In conclusion he spoke of "despairing for all journalism". Well, that was it! That was stepping over the line and I will not allow anyone to accuse me of being a JOURNALIST! Must I remind you that the only test I had to take to get this job was a height test? However, reading his letter naturally made me think about snakes, which is good, 'cause there's a WHACK of snake news right now.

First, a man in Thailand has attempted to set a world record by kissing 19 King Cobras. Now if that was me, I think I would choose something a little more enjoyable to kiss, like 19 Kings. And I'm pretty sure that there would still be a large amount of risk involved. The King of Tonga* is getting on, and from what I can tell from the picture, he's also a little on the heavy side, so there's a chance I could be flattened.

But the Thai man chose the Cobras. Well, he is a part-time snake charmer, so I'm sure he showed up with a few bottles of wine, some chocolates. I don't know if he actually set the record, but I understand he has married one of the prettier snakes after a kiss that got a lit-tle carried away.

In other reptile news, a man in Esquimalt** found a snake in his toilet. Think of the horror! You walk into your bathroom, sit down on the convenience for some serious contemplation, and when you get up and look down, there's a SNAKE in the bowl! I think the most obvious question after that shock is, "What the heck did I have for DINNER!?"

Speaking of bathrooms, a woman in Croatia recently was in hers, brushing her teeth when lightning entered her mouth, and exited via her, um, back door. Wow! Now this is something I would LOVE to have. To be able to fire lightning out your butt would be so incredibly useful. Think of all the annoying people in your life that you could take care of with one bolt from the backside. "Ma'am, you're parking meter has expired. Here's your ticket..." SHAZAM! Zapped to oblivion.

Or; "Doctor, I don't know what happened. I was berating this woman for using capital letters, and the last thing I saw was her bending over and... SHAZAM!"

---

*And may actually be dead, so still a risky and probably yucky venture.

**A community on Vancouver Island, pronounced Esk-why-malt, an old Indian word meaning "Always look in toilet before sitting down."

I'm Having a Senior Moment

I've been thinking about becoming a senior citizen. Oh, wait. That makes it sound like I'm looking for a new job:

JOB COUNCILLOR: Okay, Linda. Tell me what your qualifications are?

ME: Well, I complain to anyone about the weather with particular emphasis on it being too cold, or too warm. I monitor the lateness of all buses everywhere. When I'm driving a car, I like to back out of a driveway without looking and then I drive at a speed that is always exactly 4ks under the posted limit, however when I'm driving my electric scooter in shopping malls, I like to go as FAST as humanly and mechanically possible! And finally I phone talk shows and complain bitterly about being taxed by the government when everyone knows that the Geneva Convention Law #412, paragraph 36 Double D, sub-basement 39574 states "Any old person shouldn't have to pay for ANYTHING!"

JOB COUNCILLOR: Linda, you're in luck. We just got an opening for a Senior Citizen, you can start tomorrow!

What I meant was, we are all going to become senior citizens, as long as we look after ourselves. I know my husband is going to live well into his "Golden Years" because he takes 4,925 vitamins every day! So, when he finally pops his clogs at, say, 139 years of age, we'll know those essential fatty acids worked.

Anyway, what I'm leading to is when we reach our senior years, there is going to come a point when we will have to get rid of a lot of accumulated stuff. My mother is going through that right now. She's moving into a smaller apartment, and I'm trying to help her eliminate a lot of items, but there are certain things we get attached to as we get older. My Mom and I hit an impasse the other day over her Funk & Wagnalls. She has a full set, A to Z. I said "Okay, these have got to go." My Mom said, "No! I need my Funk & Wagnalls!" I said, "Mom, you don't need Funk & Wagnalls, you can Google."

"Google? Don't be rude! I only Funk & Wagnall!"

"Look, this is a small place. We can maybe fit in the Funk, but there is definitely no room for the Wagnall!"

"That's ridiculous! It isn't a Funk without the Wagnall!"

"Alright, alright. We'll stick your Funk & Wagnalls somewhere."

Of course, she should have those Funk & Wagnalls, because she's used to them. They're comfortable. But it made me wonder. What will I angrily refuse to let go of when I'm in my nineties, being packed up by someone half my age, who doesn't understand...

"Hey you young whippersnapper! Take you hands off my Roomba!"

Insert 'A' into 'B'...If You Dare

I read some interesting news about Ikea this week. As you know, Ikea is an old Swedish word meaning, "No two parts will fit together". Never-the-less, millions flock every day to the big box to buy furniture called 'Bjerkserk' or 'Bjorntobewild'. Why? Because the store is BRIGHT blue and yellow, so it's really easy to see!

Well, Ikea is now selling complete houses! Oh Joy! I have bought more than one piece of furniture from those fun loving Swedes, and then attempted to assemble them. Yes, your place looks great, but there will always be that one cupboard, or drawer that just never works quite right, because no matter how you tried, no matter how many different ways you held the diagrams, for some un-Odin-ly reason, it just would NOT FIT PROPERLY!!

When my husband and I purchased our first home, we needed to set up our office, so we bought a desk and filing cabinet from Ikea and enthusiastically attacked the assembly. After hours and hours of screaming and weeping, we finally got the desk together. But the part with the drawers that was supposed to hang down from the desk? There was no physical, mathematical, meteorological, cosmological or cosmetological way that thing was going to work. So finally, we sat it on the floor, where it remained for three years. Later that night, my husband's son dropped by and offered to help put the filing cabinet together. I left them to it, and a few hours later, when I went to see how they were progressing, I arrived just in time to see my stepson amputating a portion of the cabinet with a HACKSAW! "What are you DOING?!" He said, "Well, it just isn't BUILT RIGHT, and the only way we'll get the drawer IN is to saw OFF this PART!" This is a man who is now in charge of the construction of large buildings, so it can defeat the best minds.

And who was I to say he was wrong. Only hours before, I was on the verge of ramming the Allen Key into one of my *husband's* sockets because we were utterly incapable of attaching 'A' to 'B' and tightening with 'C'. So, I'm very suspicious of buying entire houses from Ikea. I should mention they are not available yet in Canada, but it's just a matter of time. They're quite popular in Finland, although Finnish police also like to pull over crooks in speeding cars by using harpoons. That doesn't have anything to do with modular houses, I'd just really like to see that. Come to think of it, perhaps having a giant harpoon handy when 'someone' is about to hacksaw a part of a house off that just won't fit right isn't a bad idea after all.

You Want Answers? I'm Full of It...Them

You've been asking for it, and so today's the day that we open up the 24 Hours Super Sack of Queries.

Dear Linda,

Lately I have become more and more concerned about my food and the fact that it keeps challenging me to do things. There's the 30 day Special K Challenge, and the two week All Bran Challenge with William Shatner, who, by the way, looks like he hasn't had a shred fibre for a few decades. Every time I sit down to eat breakfast, I'm certain my food is taunting me, possibly even laughing at me. What should I do?

Starving in Steveston

Dear Starving,

First off, if you are hearing anything other than snap, crackle and pop coming from your cereal bowl, then you should go directly to your medical practitioner and try the anti-hallucinatory drug challenge. However, I do understand your displeasure with these aggressive foods. I myself am on the 30 year butter tart challenge. Oh, you think butter tarts look mild mannered, but trust me, they don't take no for an answer.

Dear Linda,

Why?

Curious in Capilano.

Dear Curious,

If you are a man, and you're married, then the "why" is because your wife said so. Otherwise, it's global warming AND because 2 out of 3 dentists recommend it.

Dear Linda,

I was at my acupuncturist the other day and she told me that I have very large pores on my face, which she could help me with. What do you think?

Porous in Port Moody

Dear PIPM,

Here's the thing about acupuncture: the needles never go where the pain is. So, if you're knee hurts, then the needle will probably go in your elbow. Therefore I'm wondering; where would the needle go to tighten up pores? What if they stuck it in your netherlands? I can guarantee you that if someone stuck a sharp object in my private suite…the pores on my face would slam shut faster than a bank wicket at lunch time. I say go for it.

Linda,

I read last week that a pair of eyeballs was found at Sydney Airport in Australia. Is this real and if it is, what the heck is going on?

Bug-eyed in Burnaby

Dear Bug,

This is absolutely true and I'm afraid the explanation is, as usual, connected to terrorists. Safety measures have become so stringent at all airports that as of this week, when you go through security, they will now ask you to take off any metal, discard all liquids, remove your shoes, AND pop out your eyeballs! Although you will be allowed to put your eyeballs in a Zip Lock and carry them through.

Time once again to close up the Super Sack of Queries. Happy trails.

I Want Free Stuff

WARNING! This column contains words that may be disturbing to some men. Words like "gynecological", "prostate" and "hockey lockout". Reader discretion is advised.

Well it was that time of year again. The time a woman looks forward to about as much as the first bikini wax of the summer. No I'm not talking about the annual unveiling of Lloyd Robertson's* new hair colour. I'm speaking of things gynecological. Yes, it was time for my PAP test. Now PAP, as all women know, is Greek for, "Particularly Awful Procedure". And no matter how good your doctor is, and mine is pretty good, it's never less than unpleasant and yucky. That is why I strongly believe that after having subjected ourselves to these routine nasties, we should be rewarded, not just with a clean bill of health, but with FREE STUFF.

That's right. Merchandise. I don't think we get enough Free Stuff these days, and I think that getting Free Stuff could honestly start a revolution in the way people look after themselves, because then we would have a really good reason to book these dreaded appointments. Here's how it would go.

Doctor: Well, Linda, your PAP's finished. Everything looks good. How do you feel?

Linda: I feel cranky, yucky, cold and wet.

Doctor: Excellent! So we'll see you back here in a year.

Linda: Yeh, I don't think so.

Doctor: And by the way, here's your brand new George Foreman Grill.

Linda: Oh my god! Do you know how much I have wanted a George Foreman Grill?!

Doctor: See you next year?

Linda: Next year? How about next week?!

And believe me, this is the answer for reluctant men and their prostate exams.

Al: Say Ted, that's not a Black and Decker Atomic Weed Whacker 4000 is it?

Ted: It sure is Al, isn't she a beaut?

Al: Man, I would love one of those. Where'd you get it?

Ted: From my doctor, after he gave me my prostate exam.

Al: Well sign me up for a prostate exam; since there's a hockey lockout, I got a lot of Weed Whackin' to do!

I think the Free Stuff policy should also be adopted by dentists. I don't think I know anyone who actually looks forward to the dentist, and some of us have to pay real cash for the pleasure. So I think instead of handing you a lousy toothbrush and floss at the end of a session, they should give you a piece of china. Then every appointment you would get a new piece, so after 10 or fifteen years of going to the dentist, you may not have a full set of teeth, but you will have a full set of dishes.

---

*National news anchor who has been proven, through carbon dating, to be 1,436 years old.

Oh Very Young...And Mostly Stupid

My husband was embarrassed the other week. Oh, not by me. But that's always a distinct possibility. You know, big mouth, Sagittarius. You do the math. No, a high school friend sent him a letter that my hubby had written when he was nineteen. When he saw these words again after, well, several decades (but you still look great honey!) and was re-introduced to the thought patterns of himself as a teenager, he was mortified. So much so he's still curled up in a fetal position underneath the bed.

But it made me think. Could any of us survive the shock of seeing ourselves as teenagers? Sure I still occasionally have embarrassing moments...usually champagne is involved. But, when I was in high school, oh man! Let's see, there was the time I read in a teen magazine that, when applying eye make-up, you should never neglect the *lower* lid! And so I began to trowel fluorescent blue shadow completely around my eyes. I looked like a radio-active Chernobyl raccoon. Not long after, school pictures day came around. The photographer said "Nice eyes". I thought he was giving me a compliment! Years later I realized what he really meant by 'nice eyes' was, "The glow from that blue frosting is going to fry my light meter!"

Then there was the Osmond's concert. Now the fact that I was in LOVE with Donny Osmond, and so had my entire life decorated purple because that was his favourite colour is already enough to make me cringe. But they were coming to Vancouver for a show, and it just happened to land on the day that the school choir I sang in was doing a big concert. Of course, being a person of great commitment and strong moral principles, I bailed on the choir and went to see the Osmonds. I'm still not entirely sure that was wrong, 'cause, you know, I wore purple SOCKS! But every time the choir teacher mentioned *his* event, did I really have to yell, "Yes, sadly I won't be with the choir, because I'LL BE AT THE OSMONDS CONCERT, SUCKERS!!" My teacher got so sick of me he phoned my mother and told her that if I didn't clean up my act I would undoubtedly become an axe murderer, or even worse, a tax auditor.

I have more examples. Lucky for me I only have 450 words. And that's why I think that all schools today should have ESTs: Embarrassment Swat Teams. Whenever a teenager behaves like an idiot, the ESTs swing into action and erase all evidence of that behaviour, so it can't come back to bite them in their more mature futures. The Swat Team will be busy. They'll need a union. But they won't be allowed to strike, because I think we all agree, they WOULD be an ESSENTIAL service.

Love Stories

.

Batteries Not Included

Here's the biggest news I've heard in the last 6 months. London Drugs* is now selling vibrators. It's true. I read it in the business section no less. (Now kids, when you ask mommy what a vibrator is and she replies that it's a personal relaxation device that daddy sits in all day watching football, baseball and golf: also correct.) According to the gizmo spokesperson, women now want to be able to purchase these items in a more relaxed atmosphere, like a drugstore. So, this is progress? I don't think so.

First of all, let's examine history. We all know the way many men have dealt with the embarrassment of purchasing condoms at drug stores:

WOMAN: Honey, did you get the condoms?

MAN: Ahhh, no. I got this instead. I think it's a lot better.

WOMAN: What?? That's a Glad Kitchen Catcher!

MAN: Yeh, but it's heavy duty *and* it has a nice fresh scent.

And you just have to know there's going to be trouble at the check stand. Not so long ago I was in my local grocery store, and I picked up sex expert Lou Paget's book *The Big O*. (For research purposes only) When the cashier was ringing it in, she stood staring at the front cover for what I'm certain was 46 minutes and 28 seconds. To break the uncomfortable silence, I finally just had to blurt out the truth. "It's a book about OPRAH! Her life. Her times." I'm not entirely sure she bought it.

So now imagine checking out with the "personal appliance".

ME: (hypothetically, although I **know** millions of people buy them **every** day and it's **perfectly** normal) Hi, just this please.

CASHIER: (17 year old lad, many pimples) Okay…(beep) Um, it's not scanning…(beep) Nope, definitely not scanning. I'll need to get a price check.

ME: Oh for the love of Masters and Johnson, NO!!

CASHIER: (on really loud intercom) PRICE CHECK ON 2 ON THE "HAPPY JIGGLER PERSONAL PLEASURE MACHINE", THE ONE WITH THE…is that a hedgehog?

ME: …no…it's a rabbit.

CASHIER: …THE ONE WITH THE RABBIT.

And what about returns?

ME: Um…hi…um…I need to return this, it doesn't work.

CASHIER: (woman, nearing retirement) Okay…what **is** this?

ME: …ahh…it's a hand blender.

CASHIER: …oh…is that a hedgehog?

ME: No! It's a rabbit!

CASHIER: Say, didn't you use to be on television…Hey! Where're ya going? What about your hand blender?

No, no, no. If I'm ever going to purchase one of these items (and I know **trillions** of people do **every** day and it's **perfectly 110% normal**) I'm afraid I'll need it delivered directly to my door in a package wrapped with many layers of thick brown paper.

A darkened room. The internet. Now that's progress.

*Drugstore that I spend far too much money in, although not on the items discussed in this article, even though there's absolutely nothing wrong with that.

Jennifer and Brad and Me

It's time I had a little chat with Jennifer Aniston. I'm concerned about her because she just paid gazillions for a house close to Courtney Cox, so that she'd have her boney shoulder handy to cry on. What gets me is she's *still* crying over Brad. Jennifer needs some perspective and I feel qualified to give it.

Okay, Jennifer was dumped by Brad Pitt. BRAD PITT! I think we're all agreed, HE'S GORGEOUS! His face is gorgeous, his body is gorgeous, I'm sure he has warts that are absolutely breathtaking. I mean, what kind of flavour packed beef jerky would you need to keep *that* dog on the porch? Brad meets Angelina Jolie. A woman whose breasts enter a room roughly 3 minutes before she does. Angelina's looking for father material. Brad desperately wants to be a father. As a matter of fact, I believe that Angelina is carrying Brad's children at this very moment... in her lips!*

So I say there's no shame in being dropped by the handsomest man in the universe. She gave it her best shot. No, the time for tears and painful introspection is when you've been dumped by the "ARMADILLO GUY!" You see many years ago, at the radio station I worked at, I found myself being sweet talked by a plain Texan who toured North America with a bunch of armadillos.

Now in my defense, I had just escaped a relationship with someone I affectionately referred to as "DAMIEN 666!" and so I fell pretty quickly for those smooth come-on lines. You know the ones; "Honey, have you ever smelled an armadillo at sunset?" or "You would look soooo good wrapped around my Dasypodidae!" So that's how I found myself at half-time at a Lions game** at BC Place, chasing a herd of stinky armored rodents around centre field. And by stinky I mean, when you're around one, you're constantly asking "Hey, has something died?" But I did it because; well I think we all know how attractive a guy can become when he has lots and lots of armadillos.

Anyway, later that night in his hotel room, I believe just as he was about to pop the big question, "Honey, would you hose down the critters?" one of the Lions cheerleaders showed up, and before you could say "anteater relative" I was out the door! I didn't even get a chance to say goodbye to Gerry, my favourite stinky rodent. THIS is EMBARRASSMENT!

So I had to ask myself some hard, painful questions. Questions like, "Why wasn't *I* good enough for the armadillo guy?" and "What **stinks**?" So, cheer up Jennifer, because people may say to you "I'm so sorry your relationship died!" but at least they won't say "My God! You **smell** like something died!"

---

*This column was written long before anyone knew that Brad and Angelina were getting cozy. Of course, as everyone knows, Angelina has now given birth to 438 of Brad's children, and they have been recognized as a new country by the United Nations.

**Canadian football, which is different from American football because it only has 3 downs, the field is 6 miles wide, and all the players ride Skidoos.

Signs of the Apocolypso

In the extremely scientific and highly regulated world of star charts and love matches, you pretty much never see Virgo and Sagittarius trumpeted as your perfect astrological pairing. Maybe that's why my husband and I, being the contrarians we are, chose to amalgamate…just to prove it could be done with minimal lives lost.

However, there are differences between the two signs which, if measured on the Stanislackoff Scale of Severity, would register somewhere in the high 4 thousands, not counting the wind. For example, Bob always makes sure we are prepared for any disaster that could hit the Lower Mainland, i.e., earthquakes, tsunamis, volcanoes, Roberto Luongo suffering a mysterious season ending lower-body injury. So, we have emergency kits everywhere you can think; the house, the car, each of the cats have one tied around their necks, like a St. Bernard. He's always telling me that I should be more prepared for catastrophe. I remind him that I survived the great Liebfraumilch shortage of '91, so I think I can handle anything Mother Nature might throw at me. Plus, I'm a Sagittarius. When the apocalypse happens, Virgo Bob will ensure that we have all the food and supplies to keep us alive until the world is rebuilt. MY job will be to entertain folks while the hammering is going on with comedy, music and dancing. We'll have so much fun, I might even rename it Cullen's Apocalypso!

Virgo's are also big list makers. My husband always has a list going. In very busy times, I have known him to make a list of things that have to go on the list! A pre-list list. I, on the other hand NEVER make lists. The closest thing a Sagittarian comes to any sort of list, is doodling on paper. One day, Bob asked me, rather curtly, if I may say, "What's this doodle doing on my LIST??" I said, "I think the more pertinent question is, What's this LIST doing on my DOODLE?"

Our relationship almost came to a tragic end once, during The Great Butter Battle. I was in the mood for a nice cheese sandwich one day, with lots of perfectly softened butter. But when I went to the cupboard, no butter. Bob, in his organized Virgo way, had put the butter back in the fridge. So now my sandwich was going to be torn to shreds, as I desperately tried to "spread" frozen chunks of the yellow goodness. When I complained bitterly, Bob said, "Well, do you want to DIE from e-coli?" I said "YES! I do, right after I've had a tasty cheese sandwich!!" Then I whacked him in the head with the butter brick. Sadly, due to the dairy product brain injury, his only real means of communication left is lists, and I don't doodle on them. Now that's love.

Where is the Love?

I'm sure everyone will remember exactly where they were the day they heard that Jessica Simpson and that guy had split up! I was at a 7-Eleven working my way through a 640-ounce Big Gulp when I heard the news. I was so distraught, I almost couldn't finish!

What could possibly have gone wrong? Jessica and that guy seemed so happy on the millions of magazine covers they've graced over the last few years. It just makes me think that if two beautiful people who selflessly sold the TV rights to their marriage so that we could have the opportunity to see how post-pubescent millionaires live, can't make a go of it, then what hope do the rest of us have? They've asked that their privacy be respected during this difficult time, and gosh, that's the least we can do. After all, who wants the public prying into your divorce before you've had the chance to sell the TV rights to it? I'm telling you, it's the death knell for romance.

Want more proof? The Black Eyed Peas have yet another hit song out right now, and the chorus line goes like this, "My hump, my hump ... my hump, my hump, my hump." I'm sure you recognize it. The first time I heard it, I thought it was a song about Quasimodo and his, um, problem. The thing is, when

I hear someone asking me "What am I gonna do with all that junk, all that junk inside my trunk?" it's usually my husband wanting to know why I have three tennis rackets, two boxes of grass seed, dozens of empty water bottles and an entire set of Canucks bobble heads rattling around in the trunk of my car?

Is this the music of seduction? Okay, you go back to his place after a date, he dims the lights, pours a glass of wine, puts on some mood music, and suddenly someone starts yelling about humps and love bumps. When I was dating, if you got love bumps, you were sent very quickly to the doctor for some cream.

They just don't write romantic songs like they used to. You know, songs like *You Can Ring My Bell* or *She's A Brick House* or who can forget that make-out favourite *Disco Duck*? To this day, I haven't got a clue what any of them were about, but I'm pretty sure they were romantic. Yes, I know, I'm getting old.

The good news is, I hear the Black Eyed Peas are bringing out a Christmas song about Santa Claus, called *My Sack, My Sack... My Sack, My Sack, My Sack!* I *think* it's about his big bag of toys, but if I'm wrong, I sure hope there's a cream for it.

Is That a 5/8th Drill in Your Pocket?

I was watching the Women's Fantasy Channel the other day. If you're thinking 'All Chippendales All The Time' you are sorely mistaken. I'm talking about the *Home Decorating Channel*, which is just about every channel on the dial. I swear if there was a Hitler Channel, they'd have a show called *Trading Bunkers*.

Anyway, I was watching that show with the guy with the 42 inch biceps who wears overalls and not much else. (Hey! Maybe I **am** talking about Chippendales) He goes to people's houses and fixes botched jobs left by other guys who probably only have 4 inch biceps.

Here's how it goes: our hero, Bicep Man, arrives, distraught homeowner explains how they paid millions of dollars to a guy named Raoul to build them a lovely footstool. Raoul returns the next day and dumps a load of concrete in their powder room, and that's that last they see of Raoul. Bicep Man proceeds to fix the shoddy workmanship, but then something always goes wrong, and that's when he starts to whine. "Oh, man, I was just gonna blow the concrete out with 10 sticks of dynamite, but now they tell me the family dog is missing, so that means I'm gonna have to go one stick of dynamite at a time to see if we can find Fluffy, and that's a LOT of work for ME!"

Pretty well every one of these shows has someone whining about how much work they have to do. Which makes me wonder why they're so popular. Do we like watching somebody gripe incessantly about how tough life has been made for them? If that were the case, there'd be all kinds of shows filled with hockey negotiators called *I Spit On Your Offer!*

I think we keep watching because we love to hear Bicep Man say things like "I'm gonna drop that quarter round by a ½ inch to allow for the load bearing 4x8 that we'll ratchet up with the pneumatic spreader on the chance that the gasket is sitting next to the stud." Who's going to argue with that? "Oh yes, Bicep Man. You can give me the pneumatic spreader any day!"

That's why there will never be a show called *Punchline 911*, where an 'expert comedian' tries to help someone who's having trouble delivering a joke.

GUY: …and the monkey said, "Forget the bananas, look at the size of those coconuts! Ha Ha Ha."

EXPERT COMEDIAN: Well, um, you're just not funny.

GUY: Says you, Mr. **Balloon Animals**! What do YOU think Bicep Man?

BICEP MAN: We'll run PVC through the MDF and then we'll tighten up your ball-cock.

GUY: My hero!

People just respect a man who knows how to handle his tools.

Higher, Lower, Left, No Right...Yes...Yes!

My step-daughter told me an interesting story last week. She lives in sunny Los Angeles, where they are observing a week-long period of mourning over the death of Britney and K-Fed's marriage. In honour of this solemn occasion, all jeans are being worn at half-mast, and no one is playing Kevin's new CD, or is that just because it's bad, and when I say 'Bad' I don't mean 'Good'.

Anyway, back to the story. My step-daughter's apartment faces an interior courtyard and, as usual, it was a lovely day, so windows were open. As she was going about her business, she suddenly heard a woman from an apartment across the courtyard, exclaim very loudly, "OH GOD!" Now, she was certain there were no church meetings being held in her building, so her first instinct was that this person was in some sort of medical distress, and needed an ambulance, or at the very least a fire truck. However, moments later, when she heard another "Oh God!" along with some creative moaning, she realized that this person didn't need the fire department, because she probably already had the 'Jaws of Life' working on her at that very moment. So now, my step-daughter was flushing toilets, turning on fans, playing Barry Manilow music to drown out the performance (This **is** L.A. after all). But let's face it, it's very disconcerting hearing other folks having their vents blown out.

I can empathize. I've encountered this several times. The first years ago when I was holidaying in Waikiki with a boyfriend, and the couple we were traveling with were in the next room. So I'm starting to doze off, but then I hear this scream from the next room that sounded like she'd just shoved her hand in a blender. I woke up my boyfriend and told him I thought someone next door was hurt, so he pounded on the wall and yelled "Hey, do you need paramedics?!" There was no reply because, I slowly understood, all mouths were occupied. Embarrassing?

This happened again when we were living in a house, and our neighbours behind us decided to get busy 'al fresco'. The sounds that she made! To this day, the birds have not returned to that neighbourhood.

And that's why I'm worried about Singapore Airlines. They're installing giant seats in First Class that convert into beds big enough for two. I know what's coming. You're happily munching your free nuts when a desperate moan emanates from underneath a blanket across the aisle. So you hit the call button.

Attendant: Yes?

Me: I think there's a woman having a heart attack!

Attendant: Um…no she's just getting…her life vest inflated.

Then the 80 year old man next to you gives you a wink and starts to recline his seat. It's enough to make a girl walk to Singapore.

Men Versus Women

I've just completed a study of all the people living in my home, and have concluded that, yes, men and women are different.

Here's why. First: culture. For example, you, and when I say you, I probably mean me, could be in the middle of watching one of the eight or nine soap operas that you MUST watch daily for research purposes, and just at the moment when Steele is telling Cassandra he has loved her from the moment he found out that she was his long lost twin sister, three times removed, that's when your, and by your I probably mean mine, man walks in and starts making horrible groaning noises, threatening he's going to be sick unless you turn off the stupid soap, but you can't because Cassandra just told Lance she's a trans-gendered drag queen accountant.

Second: healthcare. Men now "think" they suffer because they have to have prostate exams. I tell my husband that it will never be worse than having your breasts flattened to the thickness of a crepe. Oh yes, he insists, because the doctor's entire hand, right up to his shoulder, DISAPPEARS during the exam! I checked this with our doctor, and he said yes, not only did he put his entire arm in to check my husband's prostate, but he had also stored some old files and a bunch of stuff up there that he didn't have room for in his garage.

Finally: communication. When I hang up after a phone call, I run immediately to fill my husband in on the crucial topics I have just discussed:

ME: Honey, I was just talking to Darlene, and her eyelash curler BROKE! So she had to walk around ALL DAY with one side curled and the other side STRAIGHT! And THEN, she poured SKIM milk into her coffee instead of 2% which made her feel kind of weird until she got home and emptied the lint tray in the dryer, which really calmed her down.

My husband will have an hour long conversation on the phone that sounds like this:

HIM: OH MY GOD!...YOU'RE KIDDING...NO!...YOU'RE KIDDING!...OH MY GOD!...GEEZ!...HOLY COW!... YOU'VE GOT TO BE KIDDING!...OH MY GOD!

Then he hangs up, and I wait anxiously for him to come rushing down the hall to give me the earth shattering news, but, I get nothing. So I wait, and wait. I don't want to ask, because then I'll appear needy and nosey...which I am. Finally, 6 weeks later, he'll suddenly say, "Oh, I forgot to tell you, Osama Bin Laden called. He's been hiding out all this time at Alan Thicke's* house."

So, conclusive proof, men and women ARE different. Now I've gotta run and tell my husband our doctor just called. Wants him to come in for another prostate exam...he needs his golf clubs.

---

*Canadian actor who became moderately successful with Growing Pains sitcom. Sadly for us, that show came to an end and now he keeps coming back to Canada.

Non Sequitors

Mother Teresa's Got Nothing on Me

I don't ever want to be accused of not listening to my public, so when I saw the letter in Feedback last week from Pancha Pupusera regarding my "I hate flying" column, it gave me cause to pause. Pancha suggested that I should use my journalism skills to write about things that would improve the world, things that regular human beings can relate to. I hear ya sister! What you didn't see in her letter, were a number of 'Topic Suggestions' that I could concentrate my life-enhancing comments on. Well, I don't want to let another second pass without trying to get this world on the right track. So, Pancha's Suggestion #1:

Why are cab drivers so picky? If you're downtown on a Saturday night, they say East Van is too far. What is a drunken person to do?

Good topic Pancha. I can see how this would be disconcerting for many drunks. You must understand a very important Vancouver Taxi Fact: The ONLY place a taxi in Vancouver wants to take anybody is to the AIRPORT! So when they say East Van is too far, what they are really saying is, "We'll take you anywhere you want, as long as it's the airport." There's a scientific reason for this. You see, a taxi driver's life span is only twelve hours, so they must get back to the big lot at the airport, where they were born, to fertilize new taxi driver eggs, and then they roll over on their beaded seat covers and die. My suggestion is next time you're drunk, take that cab to the airport, and then get a flight to East Van.

Suggestion #2:

Why is dating so difficult?

This goes back to the Geneva Convention, Chapter 12 Sub-Station Alpha, Species: Unknown "…whereas the less attractive must be allowed to Get-It-On!" This is an international law that decreed dating would be made so difficult and frustrating that after 10 or 12 years of going home alone, you'll take Coyote Ugly and you'll be happy about it!

Suggestion #3: **Why are people so intolerant lately?**

Most intolerance can be traced back to an e-mail chain letter written by Maya Angelou. You know the one. "Puppies are cute, babies are cute, hang-nails are cute! Now send this e-mail to 35 thousand of your closest friends in the NEXT 5 SECONDS and Bill Gates will give you his ENTIRE fortune! If you don't send it, you will die from a mysterious tropical illness that turns people into idiots, called 'The Caribbean Clap-Trap'." So, I'm intolerant of most people I meet, because I never know who might send me one of those %#!# e-mails.

Wow! Thanks Pancha! I really CAN make the world a better place! Now, where am I going to stick that Nobel?

A Historical Perspective on Petroleum

I have gas on my mind. Yes, an unusual place to have it. To be perfectly frank, or Gerry, most of the time gas usually settles in a much lower area. Perhaps it's my cooking. But today, it sits around my brain. And here's why. Was it not scant months ago that the price of gas flew up faster than an outraged cry of "Stop taking pictures of my…bad side!" from Linsday Lohan?

A litre of gas had become so expensive, folks were filling up their cars and then attempting to pay the bill with goats and chickens and children they weren't so fond of. The increase was so drastic that, of course, fuel surcharges were slapped on everywhere, leading to conversations like this:

Man: Yes, Air Canada? I'd like a ticket to Dog Leg Right, Saskatchewan.

AC: Yes, sir, that'll be $400,000.00

Man: But the flight's only 84 dollars!

AC: The rest is fuel surcharge!

Man: That's awfully high. I guess I'll get a meal included then?

AC: Are you some kind of LUNATIC?!

But now, for no apparent reason other than perhaps Madonna adopting a child from Africa, the price of gas is dropping like… well…the price of gas! Why? How are they choosing these prices? It's not a simple formula, and to answer this question, I think it's important that we look at the history of oil, in order to get some perspective.

You see millions of years ago, in the Plasticene era, there were millions of huge creatures roaming the earth that were made of a putty, much the same as Gumby and Pokey from the cartoon. Then suddenly one day (archeologists think it was a Saturday because a lot of the creatures were at the mall) there was a catastrophic event that killed them all. Best guess is a Blow Out Sale that got way out of hand.

So, they all decomposed and became oil buried deep in the ground for eons, until the 1960's when a man named Jed, a fella who lived in the mountains, had no money, in fact, he could hardly pay for food for his dependants, and then, one day he was shooting his dinner, but missed, the bullet flew into the ground, and the next thing this thick black liquid seeped up. Oil that is. Black Gold. In other words 'Texas Tea'.

Mr. Clampett became rich, so he decided to get out of the oil business and become a sit-com star. He sold his oil strike to a Texan named J.R. Ewing, who woke up one day from a terrible dream where he had been shot in his shower by an irate air traveler who was sick of paying 400,000 dollar fuel surcharges even though the price of fuel had dropped! Ha ha! Yes you're right. I made that all up, based on absolutely nothing at all. The exact same way they figure out the gas prices.

Reclaiming Youth

I'm fascinated by scientists. It may have a lot to do with the particular Merlot I'm sipping at the moment, but it may also have to do with the wonderful things they discover. For example, a few months back scientists reported that millions of years ago, apes and humans mated. The scientists also discovered that around the same time, the first alcohol was made…'cause you'd sure need an awful lot of hooch if you were going to get jiggy with a primate. I mean, all that screaming! And the monkey might be screaming too. Actually reminds me a lot of my disco days, but I digress. A few weeks ago, a big pharmaceutical company announced that their scientists have developed a drug that appears to reverse the physical effects of ageing. Now, I'm not a big fan of ageing for this reason: It doesn't matter how many crunches I do, or how much steel belting is in the industrial strength bra I wear, my skin seems to want to slide off my body via my feet and make its way, I think, to Antarctica. So when I saw this story, I got really excited…until I read HOW the pill turns back time.

Apparently it boosts levels of a hormone that is a key player in puberty. What if it actually throws us back into puberty? Oh joy! I'll be able to relive some of my finer moments. Like when one of my best friends and I were going downtown on a bus, and he had brought with him a few bananas. He decided to sit next to various folks, pull out a banana and then yell loudly into their faces "Ba-Na-Na!" I laughed until my lungs collapsed. Then there was the Whoopee Cushion incident. I was over at another friend's house, and we decided to perpetrate quite an elaborate joke on her parents. You'll love this; her parents were in the kitchen, so the two of us walked in, said hello, she walked over to the sink, picked up a full pitcher of milk, while I sat down on a chair. However, and here's the brilliant part, as I sat down, I slid the fully inflated phony gastric emitter under me, and let fly one crystal shattering, door shaking explosion of pure Whoopee Cushion wonder! My friend was so impressed with my work she dumped the pitcher of milk in the sink. I was laughing so hard inside my eyeballs just about exploded. But her parents remained stony silent, speechless in the presence of our comic genius!

Could this pill lead to packs of 70 year old men standing around a 7-11 burping the alphabet? Are we prepared to act like idiots again just to look FANTASTIC? I know I've got a hand buzzer around here somewhere.

I Can Feel it Coming in the Air Tonight

Something terrible is coming. I can sense it. No, actually, I can smell it, because like the old song says, "I'm just an olfactory girl." Yes, it won't be long before perfume will be banned in all public places.

Let's start with some history. Perfume was first used in prehistoric times by the hunter/gatherer societies. One day a cave woman was out gathering some nice shoots to go with the "Mastodon en Croute" she was planning for dinner, when she fell into a puddle of primordial ooze. Now, ooze of any kind usually smells pretty bad, but primordial was, apparently, quite the reek. So, before her hubby, Og, got home, she had the family Sabre Tooth Tiger spray her once or twice and voila!

OG: Hi honey, heyyy! What smells great? Is it soup?

HONEY: No, it's the very first perfume, and it's called Eau de Chat de Grande Dents.

OG: Wow! Can we also have it as soup?

A few years later the French put the stuff in spray bottles, because they're easier to keep on your bathroom counter than a large cat with giant tusks, and upped the price by 500 per cent. But I have to tell you, I LOVE perfume. I have ever since I was old enough to have a nose. That being said, I also understand where some of the fragrance grievance comes from. Let's just say there are some scents that are as thick and heavy as a late October fog, and there are some people who apply those scents with the subtlety of a fireman hosing down a 6 alarm blaze.

I used to do this in my disco days. I wore a fragrance to the clubs that I adored, but was so heavy you could chew it, and every time I went to the ladies room, I'd RE-LOAD! I believe my theory was not to attract a guy with my alluring scent so much as suffocate him first, and then just drag him off.

And it's not only women, men do this as well. I used to work with a fella who immersed himself in cologne, kind of like sheep dip, and you could smell him 3K before he actually arrived.

So I understand the sensitivity problem, I do, and I'm bracing myself for the ban, but let me just say this: when that day comes, that ban better include moth balls. In order to keep tiny moths away from woolens, there are people who walk the streets with clothes permeated with that noxious naphthalene smell. A smell which can kill all small animals within a 10 block radius. So when the time comes, let's be fair about the fragrance ban, or I'll be forced to really kick up a stink.

Divine Perspiration

I've decided to jump into the big debate. There sure are a lot of debates to jump into these days. There's the 'Collagen versus Bum Fat Injection' debate. My tendency would be to choose the fat from my rear 'bumper' to, say, plump up my lips or wrinkles around my eyes. My only fear is that from then on I'd always have an overwhelming urge to sit down face first. Then there's the always heated 'Hostess Gift versus No Hostess Gift' debate. This is easy; if *I'M* the hostess, go with the former.

However, I'm talking about jumping into the 'Intelligent Design versus Evolution' debate! Intelligent Design is the latest religion based theory that suggests the universe was created by God, whereas Evolution was a mildly amusing movie with David Duchovny and many slimy puppets.

Just to give you a bit more Intelligent Design back-story, it seems that many billions of years ago, God decided to have some fun and create the Universe, and then just stay out of things to see how it 'evolved', except for his keen interest in being on the side of winning football teams. Well, I'm afraid I cannot go with the Intelligent Design proposal, because I think there are far too many examples of design, where you KNOW no intelligence was involved! May I offer into evidence:

EXHIBIT A: George W. Bush. Really, I think I could rest my case on him alone, but then I'd have to fill the remainder of the column with doodles. So...

EXHIBIT B: Hummers. Even before gas skyrocketed, these vehicles were ridiculous. They're HUGE, and yet there's barely enough room for people. You could drive right over a Smart Car, and you'd never even feel it! That can't be a good thing.

EXHIBIT C: Eating Raw Oysters. You're not supposed to chew them, so what's the point?

EXHIBIT D: Deal or No Deal. I know I'm harping on this one, but, come on! There is absolutely no challenge to this show, unless you're a guy, and you're guessing the Cup sizes of the models...HEY! Let's make that the next game show. Or why not have a show where we just watch people fill in their Lotto forms, and then we'll be there, live, at their home when they don't win, again! Now that's entertainment! Finally...

EXHIBIT E: The Japanese Log Riding Contest. Have you ever seen this? Every year a bunch of Japanese people ride giant logs down a very big hill. Many get crushed. Someone should tell them about Exhibit D. It would save lives.

In conclusion, I have to go with Evolution, because the music was pretty good, Duchovny's cute and he killed the ugly alien creatures with Head 'n Shoulders. Now that's something I can believe in.

My Alternative Lifestyle

I'll give most things a try at least once. For example, a number of years ago, I attempted to give myself a bikini wax. The woman on the package was smiling, how difficult could it be? So, in the privacy of my own bathroom, I took one of the defoliating strips, slapped it onto the chosen spot, and yanked away with fierce abandon, at which point I was rocketed through the roof to the furthest regions of the galaxy, circled one or two planets, and then re-entered earth's atmosphere screaming the entire way. Three days later, once the hemorrhaging stopped, I began a support group called HAPPY; Hirsute And Pretty Proud Yo!

I've employed my let's-give-it-a-go philosophy most often with alternative medicine and therapies. Back when colon cleanses were gaining popularity, I said sign me up! Some people asked why? I replied smugly "Well, if we can put a man on the moon, shouldn't we put him on the moon with a shiny colon?" Various friends who claimed to have an excellent garden hose offered to do it for half the price, but I went with the pro, and it wasn't bad. I even managed to do the 'Flip-over' maneuver which, I was assured, can only be attempted by those who have truly gifted colons. But ultimately I did find it strange that after so many years of trying very hard to keep things OUT of that trap door, I would now pay someone handsomely to do the opposite. So, Colonics just weren't for me…in the end.

I also tried 'cupping' once. Cupping sounds like something painful that takes place in a rugby scrum, but it's actually a procedure that my Chinese massage therapist performed after suggesting I had toxins that needed to be removed from my body. So she sucked the skin of my back up into glass cups, obviously eliminating those dreaded toxins. Two days later when my husband saw my back, he asked if I had got a job as a squash court wall. I would have gone for more hickies as a teenager if only I'd known their health benefits.

So when I saw a little ad in the paper the other day for an Ion Foot Bath that draws all the toxins out of your body through your feet, I was intrigued. As you soak, the water turns a dirty colour, evidence of all the yuck leaving your body. But what happens if you fall asleep and you soak too long, and now things you NEED are draining out through your feet, like your kidneys. I have big feet, so my liver could even slide out! I'm going to pass on this one, but now I'm thinking about trying Reiki therapy…I wonder where they put the rake.

My Handicap is Me

I played my last golf game of the year a few weeks ago. Each year around this same time, I perform a very moving, emotional ceremony where I clean off my golf clubs, I carefully place each one back in their proper slots in the golf bag, gently cover them up with their Winnie the Pooh driver covers and with a small tear trickling down my cheek, I throw the clubs with all my force into my storage room screaming "I am never playing this *ratzin' fratzin'* game again!"

But the problem is, golf is a lot like the pain of childbirth. Once the winter has passed, and you hit that first sunny spring day, you miraculously forget the suffering, torture and embarrassment of the previous year, and decide to give it another try, all the while stupidly thinking that THIS go around won't be nearly as agonizing as the last.

I sometimes wonder why I ever started playing golf. I think my reasoning was this: I'm experiencing far too much joy and contentment in my life, so I must find a pastime that will foment in me a fury so strong that I may, on occasion, drive my golf cart straight into a water hazard.

When I first started playing golf, I cunningly joined two sports together; golf and sailing. So, instead of heading straight down a fairway, I would use an ingenious 'tacking' strategy. This made it very difficult for enemy golfers with anti-ballistic missiles to lock their radar onto me, due to my erratic zig zagging. Problem was, it took me 6 weeks to complete 18 holes.

There are some important things I've learned about golf, however. First and foremost, you can LOSE YOUR LIFE playing this game. Every golf course has something called a 'marshal'. The marshals drive around the course all day long making sure that everybody keeps their pace up. If you happen to get behind, and start slowing the play down, the marshal comes by and shoots you with his six gun. He will also shoot you dead if you insist on wearing golf pants that are the same colour as astro turf.

You can also lose your life trying to retrieve lost balls. In North Carolina, where I played many years ago, all the roughs at the courses were guarded by alligators! In Osoyoos*, lost balls are protected by rattle snakes. This is because the golf courses make gazillions selling lost golf balls which they purchase from the gators and snakes for discount bulk rates.

We can blame all of this suffering on the Scots. A few hundred years ago, after a bunch of them got stinking blotto from testing the first barrel of scotch, they invented golf. Someday we will have our revenge…after I buy pink golf shoes.

*Pronounced Minsk, a town in the Okanagan region of British Columbia, now famous for many excellent wineries and the mythical lake monster, Ogopogo, pronounced Minsk.

Better Than Book Learning

Summer holidays are over and school is back and for thousands of young children, these are the very first days of their formal education. They are at the beginning of years of learning and their eager, curious minds are ready to soak up all the knowledge they can get. However, there are certain topics that are not being taught in the school system, and so as a public service, I felt it was my duty to give these kids what I believe are the most important lessons they'll need in life. So listen up kids, here's

Lesson #1:

DON'T LOOK DOWN IN A PORTABLE TOILET.

Oh, you'll want to, it's human nature. You'll walk in and think, just a glance. How bad can it be? We're all human beings. Initially it's not too bad because it's usually kind of dark, but then your eyes start to focus, and slowly shapes begin materializing and you realize with horror that maybe we're NOT all *human* beings after all! But now you have to sit down, above that murky abyss, and so you go as quickly as possible, because you're terrified that any second, something will lunge up at you with it's slimy killer jaws, and pull you down through the seat into the pungent depths, never to be seen again. So, don't look down. And use the hand sanitizer.

Lesson #2:

NO ONE HAS EVER SEEN A BABY PIDGEON

There is a scientific explanation for this: they're too ugly. A baby pigeon's body is comprised of 2 parts; mouth and legs. The parents are extremely embarrassed by this, and that's why they refuse to let the general public see their offspring until they have grown into the magnificent winged creatures you see on building ledges everywhere, keeping the city safe from giant seed spills.

Lesson #3:

ALWAYS BUY THE EXTENDED WARRANTY

And when they ask, say yes RIGHT AWAY. Because if you don't, you will lose years of your life standing listening to an 18 year old with Everest sized pimples explain the many reasons you should buy the extended warranty, using a language that is totally incomprehensible, and then you'll lose another fifteen years of your life translating what he just said, and then debating the pros and cons of the extended warranty. Here's what the extended warranty does: it guarantees that once you pay for the extended warranty, NOTHING will go wrong with the purchased item until the day AFTER the extended warranty expires.

Last but not least

Lesson #4:

DON'T REPEAT YOURSELF

So, kids, when you buy your BMW 525, and you get your personalized license plate, don't put BMW 525 on the plate. It's already on the car!

Take these lessons to heart kids. I did, and look at where it got me!

But Does it Have Cup Holders?

Here's some FANTASTIC news! Last week the parent company of Mercedes launched a working concept car at Frankfurt's Auto Show, which they built so that a German tire maker who had made a 'street legal' tire that handles speeds of OVER 350 km/h could see if it really worked. They named the car Excelero. Excellento!

Now, I have not traveled too extensively around the world but, everywhere that I have visited, including other parts of this country, has speed limits of oh, 50k in the city, and roughly double that on the freeways, give or take. Yes, I know, except for the Autobahn. They are sooo lucky in Germany because on the Autobahn, you're allowed to let your speed climb to whatever the Dow Jones Average is that day. But, if you have an accident, forget what your mother always told you, you know, about the clean underwear? I promise you, it won't be clean if you hit another object traveling at Mach 6.

See, I'm just not a fan of cars that move faster than a Rene Zeilweger annulment mainly because on the one hand, I think they're stupid, and on the other hand, well, I think they're a waste of time and stupid. I really feel that too many people drive too too fast already. And what is it that everyone is in such a rush to get to? A Blowout Sale at The Brick*? Believe me, no matter what day of the week it is, you're only ever 24 hours away from the NEXT Blowout Sale!

Plus I've never been a subscriber to the "Nice Car/Drive Fast" philosophy. If somebody handed me some super hot sexy car to drive, I'd make absolutely sure I never went above 30k so everybody could see who was driving such a magnificent machine.

The truth of the matter is, there IS no street legal place to drive a street legal tire that goes 350k. I don't understand why they can't put these brilliant engineering minds to work on something REALLY useful, like a metal restaurant teapot that doesn't pour tea out of every opening EXCEPT the spout. And really, aren't 4-way stops frightening enough without adding speeds that can blast a space-shuttle out of earth's gravity?

But here's what scares me the most. I know that no matter how much this car costs, there'll be a number of guilt ridden parents with too much money who'll buy them for their teenagers as a reward for graduating without ever having torched the school. Is that a world any of us want to live in? So come on brilliant tire engineers, use your genius for something noble, like bringing peace to the world…or the Michelin Man gets it!

---

*Furniture store named after a hard object that often gets thrown through windows when someone finds out that the couch they paid the lowest price EVER for was still priced 10 times what it was worth.

I Coulda Had a V8...That Worked

Gas prices are going to skyrocket again. I know this because the oil industry reacts to any disasters that hit the planet, and we have just been rocked by another tragedy so big, I can barely stop my hands shaking long enough to take sips of my Crantini while I type this column. Yes, Paris Hilton has broken off her engagement to Paris Whatshiswhoseits. Oh, I don't really want to talk about Paris Hilton, because when one "waste of time" named Paris manages to find the only OTHER "waste of time" in the world named Paris and they decide to marry, frogs truly are about to fall from the sky. And what would they have named their kids? Louvre? Prêt a Porter? I Hate Americans? Anyway, it's over. We can all move on.

What I really want to talk about is my very first car. I was reminded of it the other week, writing about tires and people who drive at light speed. At 17, I knew as much about cars as a skunk knows about deodorant. I was so desperate to have a car that if someone had handed me a huge cow pie with 4 wheels and an antenna, and said "Congratulations, it's your new CAR!" I would have screamed (because it was the 70's) "FAR OUT!!"

But that's pretty much what I ended up with. A bright yellow used cow pie called a Maverick. Its main trouble was that you had to warm it up. Now back then, folks did spend a minute or two warming up their cars. However, if I was getting ready for school, I would have to get up at roughly 3am, start the car, then go back inside, finish sleeping, eat my breakfast, do the dishes, have a shower, write my thesis on the socio-economic affect of a flat tax system on the First World, choose my favourite Danskin for the disco that night, and THEN I would get back in the car, shift into Drive and it would cough twice, and DIE.

It also had a huge engine. So big, that over the years, 6 mechanics fell into it and were never seen again. It used to conk out completely at the worst possible moments, like on a date, parked at Little Mountain. He leans in and whispers, "Hey, wanna see my Billy Blast-Off?" (Billy Blast-Off was a toy, trust me) So I end up stuck with a loser making rocket launching mouth noises while I wait for a tow truck.

It was just the worst car. And I think it should be mandatory that everybody's first car be exactly like mine. Because when you finally get a decent vehicle, you don't care about driving faster than an F-16. You're just delirious that the thing starts at all.

Count Me Out

If I can help it, I really try not to think about the government. There are myriad other things I'd rather spend time thinking about. For example, I've spent some quality minutes in the last few days, thinking about Tommy Hilfigger and Axel Rose getting into a smack down at a ritzy club last week. Did Axel make the mistake of suggesting that Tommy try using some colours OTHER than red, white and blue in his designs for a change? And where will this lead? Helmut Kohl butts out his cigarette on Madonna's forehead because he hates her '70's flippy hair? Right on Helmut.

I also ruminated endlessly about an Alberta Cree leader who wants to give the Edmonton Oilers* a deer & moose droppings necklace to wear, for good luck in the playoffs. There's no magic involved. If the team's wearing moose droppings, ain't nobody gonna go near them.

Anyway, I only really think about the government around tax time, although it's not so much 'thinking' as just weeping uncontrollably. However, last week, the government was on my mind because of a serious crisis in our household. We didn't get our CENSUS FORM!! We were beside ourselves, because we know NOT getting your Census form sent in by the deadline leads to severe punishment. Apparently, you are taken to an underground bunker and placed in a soundproof cell, where they force you to watch *Beachcombers*** episodes for 72 hours straight. So we REALLY wanted to get our form.

For those of us with Census problems, the government very kindly set up a Help Line which we phoned COUNTLESS times. All we ever got was "You've reached the Census Help line. GO AWAY!" Okay, that's not exactly what was said, but that was the sentiment. We also went to the web site, which said call the Help Line, which then said "Are you DEAF? I SAID STOP CALLING US!"

So, because there is no alternative, and the *Beachcombers* threat is frightening , I have decided to answer the Census questions that I think the government needs to know right here.

#1: We have 3 toilets.

#2: We do not operate a farm, because our strata by-laws will only allow us to have 1 cow less than 17 inches high.

#3: I have 37 handbags, which I blame entirely on Winners.

#4: My husband has no handbags.

#5: We are in a Same Sex marriage. We have the same sex the first Tuesday of every month, unless it's a stat holiday, or the moon is waxing…or waning.

Okay, I've done my duty. If the Census Police come after us, well, I got one of those moose droppings necklaces to protect us. Sure, it's just a bunch of crap. Very much like the Census Help Line.

---

*NHL team that many years ago traded away Wayne Gretzky, and hasn't won a Stanley Cup since. It's not the Curse of the Bambino, it's the Curse of the Zamboni.

**A hokey TV series that ran in Canada for 164 years. Amazingly, the last 40 years of the show was difficult to shoot, because all the original actors were dead, so they had to prop them up a lot, but no one ever noticed the difference.

MY 'C' Cups Runneth Over

I'm a little worried about the 'Sisterhood'. Just in case you're somewhat hazy on this particular group, here's a brief history. The 'Sisterhood' was formed back in the early 70's, when, as part of the Women's Liberation Movement, many women started burning their bras. Afterwards they realized they needed to form a group that would offer unconditional support at all times. For example:

Shirley: Say Helen, I don't mean to complain, but without my bra, I've discovered that my breasts actually hang all the way down to my knees!

Helen: Shirley, you're the CEO of a major corporation. Who cares what your breasts look like?

Shirley: Yes, but it's really uncomfortable, and the other day, a big gust of wind blew them to one side and knocked a small child off his bike.

Helen: Well that's the beauty of being a woman!

And that's how the 'Sisterhood' was born. Since the 70's the Sisterhood has had a number of slogans. You'll remember "I am woman hear me roar!" and "You go girl!" and who can ever forget "Boogie Woogie Bugle...oh sorry, that's not the

Sisterhood, that's The Andrew Sisters. Anyway, I'm afraid that the Sisterhood is starting to show signs of wear and tear. May I enter into evidence;

EXHIBIT "A": Desperate Housewives.

Many of the stars of DH are women whose careers were salvaged from the Hollywood recycling bin. So you'd think there'd be some graciousness in the face of such good fortune. Sadly no. It appears the gals get along about as well as a herd of supermodels stuck in a room with one diet pill.

EXHIBIT B: Oprah.

For the season opener she had Jennifer Aniston on to discuss the "you know what". No names were mentioned because, well, the 'Sisterhood'. But then Jennifer complained that it was the MEDIA that wouldn't turn the page. (It's a shame; I just don't think Jennifer realized she was on a TV SHOW, aka *The Media*!!) And then Oprah said, "Yes, BAD media. So, Jenn, honey, sister, are you ready to start DATING again?!" Did she not just say she wanted to TURN the PAGE! And then Oprah gave everyone in the audience their own copy of Brad Pitt.

EXHIBIT C AND FINAL PROOF THE 'SISTERHOOD'S' IN TROUBLE: Bathroom Etiquette.

The other week I was waiting to use a bathroom in a small café. A woman finally exited and I entered, locked the door, and was getting down to business, when I realized there was NO toilet paper. Not a scrap. There wasn't even enough dust on the floor for me to quickly weave something soft and absorbent together. I'm telling you, if one sister can't give another sister a heads up on the Charmin situation, then the terrorists truly have won.

Self Improvement

It's Not Middle Age...It's The Crustaceous Period

The other week my doctor told me that I'm getting crusty around the edges. Kind of sounds like I've got barnacles growing all over me, which is not impossible because they like to attach themselves to things that never move, and I'm excellent at that. However, what he really meant was, I'M GETTING OLD! Now, I have to tell you that my doctor is a friend, which is why I don't get much sympathy from him. Oh, he's had the training. He's not just a neighbour who happens to have a blow torch and will happily burn various lumps and bumps off you as a hobby. No, he's a bona fide lump and bump excavator, who is also a friend. Which is something I swore I'd never do. I used to say that I would NEVER go to the same dinner parties as the man who did my Pap tests. So, I obviously had a terrible moment of weakness...or he gives REALLY GOOD Pap tests.

Nevertheless, the sad truth is I've hit that age where my body feels the need to start growing SDNs: Supplemental Dermal Nubs. The result of this is you spend a lot of your day looking in mirrors going "Oh my GOD! What is THAT?" Or "Oh JINKIES! What is THAT?" Or just "AHHHH!"

So the other week, I had this thing on my arm that first went red, and then, you guessed it, crusty. I was devastated and knew instantly that I had Arm Cancer. So I rushed off to my caring doctor, who laughed and said that it was a "Senile something or other"...or did he say I was a "senile something or other". Either way, I was well beyond my 'Best Before' date. So I had him check all the other 'mollusks' growing on me. I'm like an oyster farm, without the protestors!

And speaking of mollusks, there seems to be a shellfish theme when it comes to aging. My mother has something that grows in her throat called a Crustacean and every couple of months she'll sneeze too hard and this crusty pellet will rocket out of her mouth. And you better duck when it happens. She's already taken out one friend's eye.

Then there's the hair problem. Why, suddenly, do hairs start to grow out of places where previously no self respecting hair would be found, for example, your cheek, and then once poked through grows away from you at a record breaking speed. It's as if your body knows there's a wind storm of biblical proportions coming and you're too OLD to stay erect, so it's going to tie itself to a tree with this gross HAIR! I have a theory on why this happens, and it's...wait, what's that on the end of my nose... AHHHHHH!

Hurry Hard! And Read This

I was a little afraid to write this week's column because it might offend curling fans, and I know how dangerous curling fans can become when they're outraged and have access to a staple gun. Take my Mother. Last year when the CBC* decided to run the curling tournaments on their "Wonders of Mulch Channel" which, strangely, my Mom doesn't subscribe to, she almost choked the life out of ME, just because I used to work for them.

But I'll risk my safety in order to keep you abreast of the biggest news in curling since the Scots started throwing stones on the ice. Prior to that they threw small goats. So, in order to improve the image of curling, a number of female curlers from various countries have posed for a calendar, wearing nothing but mood lighting. They're all in their early 20's so you can imagine what they're bodies look like.

I have some thoughts on this. First, won't a naked curling calendar invite the usual high-brow comments like "Wow, look at the size of those rocks!" and "Hey! Nice brushes!" Second, why is it that whenever a group of people want to draw attention to some cause, all they can think to do is take their clothes off? Last summer there was a bunch who wanted to get people out of their cars and onto bicycles, so they had a naked bike rally. Honestly, if I'm driving in rush hour and I see a nude biker next to me, the first thing I think is *not* "Hey, I gotta stop polluting!" No, my first thought is, "Man, the things you could catch from that bicycle seat!"

Around the same time the dump truck drivers were striking for more money to cover the gas hikes. What if they had decided to use naked picketing as a strategy? Oh yes, they would have got their money in record time, but would any of us have recovered from the psychological damage?

I think the real answer to modernizing the image of curling or any sport is…Synchronized Dance. That's right. Groups of people dancing in unison. They already do this to a limited degree with football. After a touchdown, a few guys will boogie on down in the end zone. I love it! That's the only reason I watch football.

The New Zealand rugby teams do a Maori war dance before each game. That's what the curlers should do. Before the first rock is thrown, each team lines up, and they start chanting and stomping their feet, sticking their tongues out, all to the beat of the sweeping brooms. And since it's curling, we'll get MC 'Hammer' to choreograph!...uh oh...is that a staple gun in your hand?

*The CBC is the Canadian Broadcasting Corporation, funded by taxpayers, which has had numerous hit shows like *The Joys of Caulking, I Married My Sled Dog,* and *Pauline's Poutine Routine.*

Notes From Under My Spread Sheet

Warning! Parts of this column deal with the unnatural and inhumane practice of squishing sensitive body parts. If the thought of having any of your sensitive body parts inhumanely squished is disturbing to you, please go directly to page 39 where there's an excellent article on the mating habits of the nearly extinct Golden-capped Combusting Chickadee.

A few weeks back I had to go for my yearly physical, which of course, included the wonderful procedure developed by that now famous Greek man, George Strombolopoulos. I jest. I'm talking about Dr. Papanicolaou, which the Pap test took its shortened name from, thank goodness, because I wouldn't want to have to keep saying I'm going for my Papanicolaou test. Anyway, a necessary test, yes, but I look forward to it with the same kind of glee that I approach a meeting with my tax accountant. And strangely, both start off with the same opening line, "Just try to relax. This shouldn't take long."

Well, I find it almost impossible to relax when the wind is howling through your cervix, and there are instruments being used that resemble tools that strange couple in the Canadian Tire commercials used to advertise, "Look! It's a gripper AND a spreader!" I read once that back in the '70s in the early days of the Women's Liberation movement, many women started throwing down the sheets that doctors gave them, to demonstrate that they were not ashamed of their bodies or being female. I do understand that, but you know, I like having that sheet covering me. I'd really like to have a sheet covering my doctor too…as a matter of fact, I'd like everyone out in the waiting room to be covered by sheets.

And now that I am "Une femme d'un certain age" which is French for "My God! You're how old???" I'm faced with the Pap companion piece; the mammogram, which is Latin for "just how thin can we flatten your protuberances?" Another necessary procedure, yes, but I always wonder, once I'm clamped into the jaws of death and my toes have been lifted a couple of inches off the floor, why the technician feels the need to tell me not to breathe? I couldn't breathe if my life depended on it…which it DOES!

I swear if men had to have their dangling participles squished in, say, a George Foreman Grill once a year, they'd all work blindingly fast to develop something kinder and gentler. I hope I live to see all the gal's things become gentler procedures. In the meantime I'll still get it done. But I've decided that next year instead of going to my doctor for my Pap, I'm going to have it done at Mr. Lube, because at least there they give you a coffee and a free paper.

HEY! Where'd You Get Those Genes?

I wish I had grown up to be a research scientist. The reason I'm not a research scientist is because I don't know enough 4 syllable words and I haven't got a clue what a Bunsen burner is. I thought it was a wild party out at that lake.*

My best friend's daughter is 13 and I already know she's going to be a research scientist, because she quite regularly and without any regard for those closest to her, tosses around words like tracheotomy and duodenum. She would have no problem explaining her findings. I would probably say things like "Okay, the thingy divided in two, and that was really neat, and stuff like that."

Luckily for me, to get hired to write a weekly column in my paper, they only require two things: 1) I know how to spell columnest…colimnust…sorry, columnist. And, 2) I promise not to use italics *too much!*

However, research is important. Thanks to research we now know it's a gene that is responsible for addiction to shopping at Winners.** (Yay! It's not *me,* it's my *genes!* Speaking of that, you gotta see these FAB Miss Sixtys I got for 3 cents!!)

The thing is, research scientists can score some serious change if they come up with something really good to research, like the bunch in Liverpool who have just released the results of their study, which is: 1 out of every 25 fathers are unknowingly raising children that are not theirs.

So, given the thousands of incurable and unsightly rashes that need creams invented, why would they pick this crucial issue to apply their large brains to? I think it went like this:

(SCENE: laboratory cafeteria)

Researcher 1: Hey, did you hear about Norm?

Researcher 2: No.

Researcher 1: He just found out that his son, Mbatumbe, isn't his.

Researcher 2: Bummer…hey, maybe we can get a big fat grant and find out how many schmucks there are like Norm around the world.

Researcher 1: Great idea!

And who paid for this study? My first guess is the International Milkman's Association. They're motto, "Fresh Milk Delivered to Your Door…and Fresh Sperm!" They probably wanted to get some official tally of their members' contribution to the lonely housewives of the world. Then I thought, maybe it was Prince Charles. Maybe he wanted to be reassured that he wasn't the only guy staring into the face of a child who looked suspiciously like a former polo team mate.

And so, after studying vast amounts of data, and I suspect, using a Bunsen burner or two, the researchers concluded that nearly all of these children were the results of, no, not faulty genes, but EXTRA-MARITAL AFFAIRS! You're kidding!! Hmmm, maybe I could've been a research scientist after all.

*That lake is spelled differently than Bunsen of the 'burner', however if you're at a wild party there, you really don't care.

**In the U.S. it's TJ Maxx. Different name. Same addiction.

Come On, Take a Pill!

In this strange and uncertain world we live in, it's reassuring to know that someone, finally, has developed the first 'anti-stupidity' pill. Hans-Hilger Ropers at the Max Planck Institute for Molecular Genetics in Berlin, reports he's had encouraging success testing the pill on mice and fruit flies. (I believe Mr. Ropers came up with the idea for an anti-stupidity pill at a really WILD Oktoberfest a few years back, right after someone poured a keg of Warsteiner down his lederhosen) You may very well ask how you can tell a fruit fly is being stupid? According to Dr. Ropers, it's pretty easy, because the Drosophila Melanogaster, which is Latin for "Who left this banana rotting on the windowsill?" does a lot of stupid things.

For example, there are a great many fruit flies that spend loads of time hanging around on items other than fruit. This is definitely frowned upon by the fruit fly elite. Stupid fruit flies also have a tendency to shoot pop through their noses, and get tattoos of their girlfriend's or boyfriend's name. However, once they were given the anti-stupidity pill, this behaviour, for the most part, ceased.

Now, as with many new drugs, there are certain groups lobbying for the anti-stupidity pill to be released early, without being fully tested, for compassionate reasons. The largest lobby group, Mel Gibson's wife and his 18 thousand children, are desperate to get the pill right now*. They claim that if they can get Mel on the drug immediately, it'll eliminate the possibility that he'll get drunk again, or that he'll ever do another M. Night Shyamalan movie. A relief to us all.

There's a group that wants to give the anti-stupidity drug to Paris Hilton, but Dr. Ropers says he can't manufacture the large amount of pills needed. Tour de France Chump-ion Floyd Landis denies that he has EVER used ANY anti-stupidity drugs. He insists that he comes by the dope in his body naturally. No arguments there, Floyd.

Finally, there's a group asking for early release of the anti-stupidity drug in England. They want to give the pill to Heather Mills McCartney, so that she will come to her senses, take the 30 million Pounds she's been offered by Paul, and put a stop to the endless variations of *You Say Goodbye, and I Say Hello* being used in headlines. As you know, the Mills/McCartney divorce turned ugly last week, after Paul locked Heather out of their London mansion. Paul's legal team claimed she doesn't have a leg to stand on. Mills said that was because she'd left it in the garage leaning up against the furnace! I hear she was hopping mad.

So what's next for Dr. Ropers? An anti-tasteless joke drug. Don't worry, I'll be his first test case.

*After Mel Gibson's drunken anti-semitic tirade, he completed rehab, and then sent a nice arrangement of kosher flowers to every Jewish person in the United States. And as a real display of his contrition, he re-edited his film *The Passion of the Christ* so that Jesus doesn't actually die, he just goes to Disneyland.

Excerpts from Madame Ovary

WARNING! This column may be disturbing to some men of the male persuasion, due to the fact that the word "period" might be used in a sentence that has NOTHING to do with the end of a segment of a hockey game. In order to avoid any psychological damage, please close this paper now, and discuss one of the following topics with other male persuaded types:

a) Top 10 power tools of all time.

b) BBQ disasters I have lived to talk about, or

c) The joys of pressure washers.

This is the second installment in an ongoing series about aging that I will be writing mostly when I get sick and tired of aging. Today's topic, Menopause.

There was a time in my life when I was convinced that I would be the exception to the aging rule. I was certain I just would not experience the various and sundry aspects of growing old that everyone else does. You know, gray hair, wrinkles, failing eyesight, sudden and inexplicable appreciation of today's soft hits and yesterday's even softer favourites.

I would sail into my 90's looking say, 40ish. And scientists from all over the world would visit me wanting to know my secret to the fountain of youth. And I would tell them, GUM! Yes, chew lots of gum! No, that would be a joke, because there would be no secret. I would simply be some magical freak of nature.

Much to my chagrin, I have discovered I'm an ordinary human being. My latest proof? Menopause! Of course, I thought I'd coast through and hardly notice it. I'm delusional, because my period has been arriving for over thirty years with practically every option available; pain, headaches, zits, bloating, weeping. Oh the weeping.

Barista: Would you like whipped cream on your Mocha?

Me: Whaaaaaaaaa!!!

So hormones are percolating again and with that come headaches, even more shocking bloating, and a renewed attack of zits that have an average size of a VW Bug. Can't tell you how THRILLED I am to have those back. Oh well, a gigantic pimple in the middle of my forehead will draw people's attention away from the fact that I'm STILL weeping uncontrollably.

But here's a Menopausal morsel I wasn't expecting. I think my hair is falling out. WHAT THE #!*$! Now, I have a lot of hair and hairdressers have told me many times that I'll never go bald. But there's so much coming out right now, I've started collecting it so I can knit myself a toque, just in case. And hot flashes are on their way. I look forward to them the way I look forward to a root canal.

No, it won't be long until I am one giant, bald, sweating, balloon shaped pimple listening to Air Supply and...weeping. Please send your sympathy cards to my husband, Bob.

The Great Slide of '07

Here's an example of one of the things I hate about aging; visible shadows at the corner of your eye. You see, when I was much younger, I occasionally spotted some sort of fuzzy shadow on my face through that peripheral vision we all have. And so I would just remove it. Usually it was a fluff, or a giant chunk of Maybelline mascara that had broken off my oh-so-natural looking eyelashes.

These days, being almost past my expiration date, I'll see some "thing" on my face out of that peripheral vision, but when I grab it, I realize with terror, that I'm grabbing ME! What I thought was an innocent fluff sitting on my cheek is some lumpy growth that's actually on my forehead, but my forehead has now slid down to where my cheek used to be. And I can't let go because I won't accept that it's attached, so now I'm screaming as I keep yanking ME, plus the rest of the people in the crowded elevator are screaming because they think I'm trying to rip some crazy Cronenburg-like monster off my face.

And that's why I use anti-aging creams. I think the odds that any of them really work are about as good as the odds of Marcus Naslund* winning a Nobel Prize for Giddiness. However, I can't take any chances, so I use them…all of them. I have so many things I put on my face at night, by the time I get them all applied, the cats are bugging me for breakfast!

Plus there are thousands of products to choose from. There's a cream that "fights dullness". They should send a truckload of that stuff to Stephen Harper. There's another cream that "repairs intolerance". Intolerance? Then there's a "unifying" cream. I guess that's for skin that wants to separate to form its own independent face, but still wants to maintain the monetary system of the original face.

There's yet another cream that fights "electromagnetic waves". I had no idea that electromagnetic waves were hitting my face, but I think that may explain why I pick up The Weather Channel in my head when I wear hoop earrings.

Sometimes I'll buy a skin product just because I like the packaging.

"Say, Linda, your face is glowing, what are you using?"

"Oh a wonderful purple jar. I've never used a purple jar like this before. And it matches my shower curtain."

It's such a battle. I need to de-puff my eyes, and re-puff my lips. Perhaps in 10 years, my puffy eyes will have slid down to my lips. Problem solved. I just hope my lips don't slide any further down, because if I think I see a fluff on them, and start yanking at it, I could get arrested.

*The underperforming star player on the Vancouver Canucks who has since been traded to New York was much criticized for always looking miserable. After extensive medical tests it has now been revealed that he was wearing the wrong size jock strap.

Decorate THIS, Martha!

I contributed to the Martha Stewart Rehabilitation Program the other day. I know that sounds like there was some woman dressed in an Armani suit, with her designer Shar-Pei called Yum Yum, Dum Dum, or Poo Poo, standing outside the liquor store, holding a can and asking for spare change. But no, I just bought one of her new and improved magazines.

I'll admit it now; my name is Linda, and I'm a decorating magazine-a-holic. (Hellooo Linda!) But you know, I've never really enjoyed Martha's, so it's always been strictly fall-back if I'm on a long flight, or ferry ride and I've bought every other magazine available, including the *Decorating with Dead Skin and Ear Wax Quarterly*. I usually get to the end of Martha's and say, "I don't have time to sew seashells onto the waistbands of my husband's underwear, so why do I keep BUYING this thing!" Why? Because of the immense pressure that Martha exerts on us. The pressure to have every inch of our lives gilded and embroidered and CLEAN, for crying in the sink! And the gods know I've tried. When the "romantic beds" became fashionable, with the thousands of pillows piled on top, I joined the crowd. Then people would visit.

"What a beautiful bed to sleep in!"

"Oh, we don't actually SLEEP in it! I'll never get the pillows back in the right order."

I'll tell you when I threw in the cross-stitched linen hand towel. We were having dinner one night with our friends, who I'll call Bob and Petra, because, well, those are their names. Petra is a wonderful decorator, and they have a beautiful home. However, I walked into their office, and there, sticking out of the garbage can, was a giant red daisy! No garbage in the 'garbage' can, just the daisy. I cried, "Okay, I surrender! I can not keep up!" While Martha was in court and then in jail, I came across a number of women who felt that the government had purposefully gone after Martha. They're absolutely right! But not because of insider trading. Every man in the FBI, the judge, the men in the jury wanted to "get" Martha because they were sick to death of being told by their wives, "Don't put THAT tablecloth out! It doesn't match the daisy in the garbage can!!"

And the pressure is about to return. On her television show, I once saw Martha, and I swear on my stack of *Architectural Digests* this is true, take a poached egg out of the water, and then with scissors, trim the edges. I'll give you a moment to let that sink in…she TRIMMED an EGG with SCISSORS! Surely that's a hangin' offense!

Basic Training

I wish I was a better person. If I was a better person, I'd probably enjoy watching all 800 spin-offs of CSI, and I'd learn valuable things about investigating crime, like, it's better to be solving murders in Miami than New York, because the weather's nicer, and there're lots of pink buildings. Also, David Caruso never lets himself be upstaged by corpse-eating worms, and I think that says a lot.

But here's where I really, really wish I was a better person: excercising. I've known people who can't start their day without blasting onto the streets for that refreshing early morning run. I can't start MY day without being hooked up to Tim Horton's* life support. Even so, I still begin every day thinking that I WILL get my workout done. I think like this partly because I've had too many chocolate sprinkles, and also because in my mind, I see myself as a pretty athletic person. Kind of the way Madonna sees herself as an actress.

I've tried them all: Aerobicize, Step, Yoga, Pilates. A while back I bought a Tai Chi video, because it seems to help a lot of people, and it's slow enough that you could do it while holding a cappuccino. So I stuck the tape in and began. First, Awakening Lotus, then onto Bending Willow, through to Disconcerted

Warrior and Itchy Flamingo, after which you had to spin around to face the opposite way, so now I couldn't see the TV! I shut it off and finished my coffee.

I buy all the stuff. A few weeks ago I bought a big exercise ball, but by the time I got it pumped up I was exhausted and had to rest for 5 or 6 days. Then I bought these pod things that have little knobby bumps on one side. I *think* they're for some kind of exercise. It's also possible they're an alien life form lying in stasis waiting to attack after I've become inert from a Tim's** overdose. Who knows?

My latest purchase is a YogaLates book. As you can guess, this is a form of medieval torture that combines Yoga and Pilates. But I'm going to be really honest with you. From a spiritual, scientific and dermatological standpoint, I am against any exercise that gets you twisted into such a position in which you can actually see your own end coming!

So, I just throw all this stuff into a box and once a week, I lift the box up, and put it down again. Whew! What a workout. Time to go and get one of those grandé YogaLattés, hold the whipped cream…oh what the heck, gimme the whip! I'll lift the box twice tomorrow.

*Maker of coffee and donuts, loved by every man, woman and cop in Canada.

**See above

Sasquatch and Other Beasts

Give Me Big Foot Any Day

At long last! There's new Sasquatch footage. I have not been this giddy since Glen Clark* became a capitalist. So like billions of other Canadians, I tuned in anxiously to see the long awaited incontrovertible evidence that the hairy giants really do exist. Well, other than those guys from ZZ Top. And hallelujah, the footage was, you guessed it, BLURRY! You'd think with the advancements in video camera technology, with all the stabilization doo-dads, and super duper zoom what-nots, that it would be impossible to make Big Foot fuzzier than he already is.

However I don't doubt the sincerity of the Manitoba fella that took the footage. After all, he did hire a renowned Big Hairy Creature expert, who after carefully viewing the film for a good long minute or two, came to the unshakeable conclusion that "It is either a human or a sasquatch, but among those two candidates it is not clearly one or the other, due to the blurriness of the footage." Well, if that's not a ringing endorsement, then I'm a 9 foot primate's uncle.

And so, with bona fide Big foot video in their hands, the Manitoba cinematographer's mother did what any mother who wants to advance the scientific investigation and understanding of the shy creature would do...she cut off access to the video and opened it up to the highest bidder. After all, mothers innately know how to handle large primate situations. If I had a nickel for every time *my* mother said to me during my dating years, "Don't you bring that baboon around *here* any more!"

Fox News was the highest bidder, somewhere in the 6 figures range, which makes sense since they already have one big ape working for them named Bill O'Reilly. But let me just state right now that I am Pro-Sasquatch because I think they have to be the most intelligent beings on earth. After all, they've maintained their secrecy for a few thousand years, only coming out of hiding when a new Jet Li movie is released.

And they are also peaceful creatures. You never hear about Sasquatch wars, or even Sasquatch skirmishes. I also think it would have been great to have Big Foot in last week's provincial leaders debate. Not for his different views, because except for the fact that he *doesn't* want to save the Grizzly because they *eat* sasquatch, his platform's pretty much the same as the Green Party.

No, it would be great because once you became brain petrifyingly bored with hearing the same old lines repeated over and over again by the leaders, you could keep yourself amused by looking for bugs and crap in Big Foot's fur.

*A far-left-wing premier of British Columbia, who went to work for the biggest capitalist billionaire in Canada. He was only able to do this after having socialist by-pass surgery, covered, of course, by our universal health care.

Aliens Have Landed

I believe that aliens walk among us and are preparing to take over the world. Now I know you will say, "But Linda, this isn't news. Liza Minelli, Michael Jackson, Richard Simmons. They've been walking, sometimes staggering, sometimes even bouncing among us for years!" Point taken. But I think that bona fide aliens wouldn't be that obvious, or embarrassing. So after serious consideration, I have concluded that Liza et al are not aliens, they're just CRAZY!

Serious invaders would be far more surreptitious. They would wear us down from within, to such an extent that when the hordes arrive on takeover day, we'd be so dazed and exhausted, it would be a relief just to have someone else take control, even if that someone does have 12 heads and green goop oozing from 18 large orifices. That's why I believe until that day arrives; the aliens disguise themselves as CATS! I know this, because I am being held hostage by two of these intergalactic monsters.

Here's how they're doing it. First: exhaustion. When they sleep with me they organize themselves so that they pin me in, one on each side. That way, I am unable to move for many, many hours, at which point my legs have become so numb they could actually chew them right off me, and I wouldn't feel a thing.

Then, when one gives the signal, roughly 4:30am, the other goofy goof-ball one goes out in the hall and very loudly starts to sing what I believe are all the most famous arias. And so even if I could get back to sleep after the leg amputations, this behaviour makes that impossible.

Next step: messing with your mind. Example: food. What is a perfectly acceptable chicken banquet breakfast, becomes possible poison at dinnertime and must be avoided at all cost. So you always have 84 cans of food open in the fridge. Also, if the state of the litter box is not exactly to one of our cats liking, he will happily leave his download just outside the entrance. And so I plead with him, "How many times do I have to tell you, it's THINK outside the box!" But he just gives me that look that says, "You know, I am a superior being!"

And he's right, because I can tell exactly what position he held on the spaceship. Because he's so serious, I know he was the ship's Captain. The goofy goof-ball? Well, it's pretty obvious he was the in-flight entertainment.

I know Armageddon is nigh. They're all here. I see them every time I visit Petcetera's Alien Adoption Room. And the Captain has ordered me to bring home the ship's therapist, because the in-flight entertainment is driving him nuts with the arias! Resistance is futile.

How Much is That Dolce Doggy in the Window?

It doesn't take much to distract me. That's why I've spent most of the day, slack-jawed, staring at snowflakes falling from the sky, immobile, until my husband finally shook me and yelled loud enough so it would register somewhere in my dormant subconscious "Snap out of it! You've got a duty to the commuters of the Lower Mainland to write down your most inane, superficial, bone-headed thoughts in your column!" I suddenly came to. "YES! I mustn't forget my duty…um, why is that again?" "Because you get paid!" "Oh, right."

So, inane thought for this week: I was in the Bay* the other day and I spotted their doggy fashion section. Everybody's selling doggy clothes. I swear if you went into Ocean Cement to buy some concrete, they'd have a doggy clothing rack too. So I had a look.

There were the usual raincoats, and sweaters, but then I saw something that made me question the overuse of electroshock therapy. A doggy bathrobe. A bathrobe…that a dog wears. Now I know that dogs like certain things. For example, I have never met a dog that didn't like having his bum scratched. In fact, many men I have known enjoy the same thing. When I do it for my husband, his right leg starts pounding the floor, it's so cute.

Dogs also love to get together with other dogs as often as possible so that they can sniff each others', um, "back 40". Come to think of it, many men I have known…well, never mind that for now. Finally, I know a lot of dogs, upon finding a steaming mound of something downloaded from, well, ANY other living thing, will happily chow down. But I'm trying to imagine at what point in the day a dog might stop licking his dangling participles and say to himself, "Man, would I love to slip into a bathrobe right about now." They're also selling booties for dogs. I'll tell you where a dog needs booties. In the ARCTIC! Because it's minus 3 THOUSAND degrees, and that's without the wind. I guess I'm just a canine fashion rebel. I was once kicked out of a doggy dress-up shop in Toronto, because I picked up something that had baubles and feathers and sparkly things and commented to my step-daughter that "this would be demeaning for her Boston Terrier". The woman running the shop spat back with venom that it would NOT be demeaning. Well, for Richard Simmons' dog maybe. I think she was wearing a thong two sizes too small, because who in their right mind could take this stuff seriously!

Look, I can't start dressing a dog for Vogue covers, I can just barely get MYSELF dressed in the morning. And what if it starts…oh look, snowflakes…isn't…that…beauti….

*World's oldest department store. Held the first white sale immediately after man invented the wheel, making it much easier for delivery.

A Peeka-Boo-Boo

These are the Dog Days of Summer. The Ancient Greeks coined this phrase when it got so hot during the summer that their dogs started to spontaneously combust. So I thought I'd tell you a happy summer story called *How I Almost Killed a Dog.*

This past June my husband and I were in Toronto for a visit and we agreed to baby sit two dogs for a few days, which meant we got to stay in a nice house at no charge. Good deal. The dogs' 'mum' told us that one of the dogs, Peeka, had a 'ball obsession' so we should keep an eye on her and make sure when we're playing fetch, she stops before she gets to the point of exhaustion. "No probs" we said "This'll be fun!"

After her owner left, Peeka wanted to play ball right away, but it was 350 degrees with the humidity, so we told her "Later". Now, Peeka is what I call a 'spare parts' dog. She's part Yellow Lab, part Corgi and I think, part Martian. She's the size of a Lab, with legs that are about 3 inches long. I think she's a little embarrassed by this, but she disguises it well.

So, once it cooled off, I grabbed one of those plastic ball-whipper things, and I started to wing the ball to the back of the yard, and she took off the way a really strange looking alien dog who is ball obsessed would. But she was fast and, yes, she LOVED chasing the ball. Plus, she always brought it right back! So I concluded she was a very SMART alien.

The one thing her owner didn't mention was an actual time limit. We were only at this for somewhere between 5 & 10 minutes when I told Peeka "That's it. No more." She paused for a moment, clearly betrayed and then she started to stagger around the garden and shortly after that she just fell over sideways, gasping for air. I ran to her and I think in between her gasps I could hear her saying, "Call 911!"

I frantically called her owner, and while her phone was ringing I was picturing headlines in the paper, "CANADIAN COMEDIENNE KILLS CORGI CROSS! PRIME MINISTER PROMISES PAINFUL PUNISHMENT FOR PUNCHLINER!" By the fourth ring, Peeka was coming around so I hung up, got the dog to the water dish, and eventually she cooled down.

I couldn't believe it, I had only been there for a couple of hours, and I'd just about killed this dog! I felt terrible, I had to make it up to her, and so I bought her a new car. Those short little legs can't reach the gas pedal. But it has air, so she will stay cool.

Enraptured By the Raptors

Have you been watching the "Eagle Cam?" If not, you may be the only one. The live eagle nest website has got to be the most popular site in the world right now, if you don't count the 'Ryan Seacrest and Paula Abdul Kiss and Make Up' site, or the 'George W. Bush Actual Completed Sentences' site. So, like tens of millions, I have been sitting for hours, watching eagles sitting for hours, on eggs, as they wait for the pitter patter of little bone crushing talons around the nest. You may already know this, but unlike human babies, baby eagles are not delivered by the stork, because the parents tend to eat the storks immediately after the delivery.

Anyway, after spending many, many hours watching and waiting for the blessed event, I have learned a few very important things. The first being, there is absolutely NOTHING to watch on television! As interesting as the Eagle Cam is, there are so many people trying to watch, that it can't keep up, and so the picture gets stuck regularly, and just as often, goes black for long gaps. And I find that infinitely more entertaining than anything I can get on TV!

Oh, I can already hear your indignant cries, "Are you kidding?! What about *Deal or No Deal?*!!" Well, who can argue that a game show where skillful contestants must SIMULTANEOUSLY open their mouths, force air through their vocal chords, run electrical impulses through their brain and then yell out a number between 1 and 26 isn't riveting entertainment? But I'll still take the black screen.

I have also learned that watching these eagles really takes your mind off the troubling news of the world. For example, there was a story last week about scientists who have developed a bean that won't cause gas. In this age of skyrocketing fuel prices, is this not a missed opportunity? Shouldn't they be developing a car that has some sort of hose affair you could attach to *your* 'tail pipe', after having a heaping helping of Heinz beans in tomato sauce? Then your own internal combustion can fire your vehicle's internal combustion all the way to, well, I think one 14oz. can will get you to Cranbrook.*

Finally, if you're thinking about gifts for the new eagle parents, I've learned they DON'T want diapers. But, Mum has had her eagle eye on one of those jogging strollers. This live 'Eagle Cam' has become so huge, not surprisingly, the whole idea is expanding. Apparently Brad Pitt and Angelina Jolie have rejected a 'Birthing Cam' site for their imminent arrival. However, Paris Hilton already has a few 'Conception Cam' websites. Now that's something that might drive me back to Howie Mandel.

*A small town in British Columbia that has a river filled with 'cran'. You can never get too much cran in your diet.

A Conversation With My Cat

I'm nursing an invalid cat at the moment. Here's what happened; I had inadvertently left doors to a big closet that holds the built-in vacuum canister open, so while I was getting the vacuum hose sorted out in the living room, Nelson, the deep thinker, in a rare fit of adventurousness, decided to poke around forbidden territory. Then I turned on the vacuum from the living room, and it fired up in that closet and his legs must have spun like Wyle E. Coyote trying to escape one of his own bombs. Unfortunately in his hasty exit, his back foot hit a piece of sharp metal stuck in the floor, and it cut his foot AND I was to learn, a tendon.

After an hour of microscopic surgery and an overnight stay at the doc's, his leg is completely bandaged, he's wearing the 'cone of silence' so he looks like a furry walking satellite dish, and my dream of a late summer Alaskan cruise has vanished quicker than a mole on Sarah Jessica Parker's face. So, while he recuperates, he and I have been watching a lot of T.V. together and as usual, he has many, many questions:

NELSON: Why are we watching SO much HGTV?

LINDA: Because I'm trying to get tips that will make the place look great.

NELSON: Well, here's a tip, why don't you iron that Mount Everest of laundry that's taking up half of my healing couch?

LINDA: Yeh, yeh. Okay, you don't like HGTV, how about CNN? Oh look, it's McCain/Obama coverage.

NELSON: I do not understand the American electoral system.

LINDA: That's because you're a cat.

NELSON: *You* understand it?

LINDA: No, but that's because I'm a human being, who doesn't have a degree in quantum physics and hanging chads.

NELSON: I knew a dog that got kicked in the hanging chads once. He never seemed quite the same after that.

LINDA: Understandable, but different hanging things.

NELSON: So, how does it work?

LINDA: I think the jury's still out on whether it does, but, look, all I know is if there's a problem, it goes to the Electoral College, and they throw a 'kegger' and when everyone is good and drunk, they pick a winner.

NELSON: Listen, could you do something for me?

LINDA: Switch to Animal Planet?

NELSON: No! I got an itch behind my ear I can't get.

LINDA: Oh sure, there?

NELSON: Higher...higher...left...ahhhhh! Thanks. Okay, I've had enough politics, what else is on?

LINDA: We could watch Ben Mulroney trying to appear amusing in a scripted yet completely spontaneous and amazingly hip manner on Canadian Idol.

NELSON: Linda, I've got stitches in one leg, my head is in a bucket and I am incapable of licking my privates...don't you think I have suffered enough?!

Of Ungulates, Un-Holy Sightings and Unhappy Campers

Llamas, chocolate Marys and letters about grumpy Vancouverites. Three things that appear to be completely unconnected…or are they? Cue dramatic music: Dum Dum Dum DUMMMM!!

Let's begin with the llama. Last week there was a 'rogue' llama on the loose in Pitt Meadows*. People were warned not to approach him because he, apparently, was spitting mad, and I mean that literally. I wondered what could possibly get a llama so riled up. My first thought was the hot real estate market. He had probably been out looking for a nice little starter dung pile with his agent, and when he found the perfect corner in a pretty Pitt Meadows field, close to schools, for ONLY $350,000, no doubt he covered his agent with one mighty gross goober.

Believe it or not, you can tell how upset llamas are by what's in their spit. If they're really mad, they'll snort it all the way up from their third stomach, where the goop has had plenty of time to ferment. I think when it comes to paying for real estate in Metro Vancouver, we all wish we had third stomachs.

By the way, the llama is a chocolate colour! Dum Dum Dum DUMMM! Workers at a chocolate factory in Fountain Valley, California, found a column of chocolate drippings they claimed looks like the Virgin Mary. A couple of things. First, if the V.M. was going to make Herself appear in something, why would She choose a blob of chocolate? Or a ham sandwich? Or a bird dropping on a window? Why wouldn't She save all Her energy and show up on stage during the half-time show at the Super Bowl? Then again, maybe She already has. I'm certain that when Janet Jackson flashed her right headlight on that infamous day, millions of male football fans had a religious experience.

Second, I've looked long and hard at the picture of the chocolate lump, and I definitely do NOT think it is the manifestation of the Virgin Mary, and anybody who believes that obviously needs their medication adjusted. No, in my mind there is absolutely no doubt that the chocolate lump is nothing more than a manifestation of DAVID DUCHOVNY! Dum Dum Dum DUMMM.

You'll remember that when David was living here while he was shooting The X Files, he made a crack on the Letterman show that it's always raining in Vancouver. This was a blow to all Vancouverites, who frequently had offered David shelter from the downpour under their giant golf umbrellas. Many of them are still in therapy dealing with the betrayal. Now, thanks to Global Warming, we have beautiful weather ALL the time. But David's gone and in his place, millions are moving here from the east. And THAT'S why Vancouverites are grumpy. Dum Dum Dum DUMMM!

*A suburb of Vancouver named after Brad Pitt, which is just about big enough to hold all his children.

Polly Want A...Better Family!

This is a very difficult time of year. Stores are jammed, traffic is crazy, and they're going to drag the Rita McNeil* Christmas Special out yet again. Who needs that? But the number one reason it's difficult is because in the next two days, at some point, you will have one frantic hour left to try and find the 'perfect' gift for that loved one. Please, take my advice. When that moment arrives, no matter how tempting it may be, do NOT purchase a small PARROT! Here's why.

Trying to find the perfect Christmas gift for my Dad was like trying to find a millimeter of loose skin on Joan Rivers' face...scientifically impossible! So one year, faced with the same desperate challenge, after 2 or 3 long seconds of thought I said to the frightened woman sitting next to me on the bus, "HEY! My Dad does claim to be a bird lover, so what better gift for a bird lover, than a small, really, REALLY loud parrot?" And that's when the thin ice formed, and I blithely walked onto it.

You see, at that moment, you just don't consider that the reason a person doesn't already have a really LOUD small parrot, is because they DON'T WANT ONE. So really, it would have been no less shocking to them, if I'd shown up on Christmas morning with a large marine mammal.

DAD: Oh boy I'll bet it's slipper soc…no, wait…it's a…dolphin?

LINDA: Whaddaya think Dad?

DAD: The carpet's all wet!

MOM: This is very nice dear, but we have no ROOM for a DOLPHIN!

LINDA: Come on. What about that big bathtub upstairs?

MOM: And we're going to Vegas next week, who'll look after it?

LINDA: Well, I can't, my strata doesn't allow dolphins. Harbour seals yes.

DAD: I don't remember ever asking for a dolphin.

LINDA: I know! But you always said you love ocean creatures!

DAD: I said I like to eat fish!

Well, long story short, they did keep the bird for awhile, until the day it became clear that there was a mouse in the house. We think he was a gang mouse, because after finding a little bit of blood on the bird, we realized the rodent was climbing up into the cage and beating the 'down' out of the parrot for the sunflower seed loot.

And that's when I had to correct my error and find a new home for the really, really LOUD small parrot. Which I did, and I'm sure he's living a happy, screechy life to this day. Anyway, I learned my lesson. I do not buy animals for Christmas presents any more. This year, I HAVE found the perfect gift. I'm getting all my loved ones that car alarm, the one that cycles through about thirty different ear piercing sounds? I can't wait to see the looks on their faces!

*Canadian singer famous for singing *Working Man* with Cape Breton coal mining choir the Men of the Deeps. Not to be confused with the exotic dance show called Rita McFeel and the Men Going Deep.

The Gull Whisperer

And now, Episode 2 in the mini-series titled *Linda; Queen of the Jungle*. You'll remember in Episode 1, Linda attempted to kill the wild tennis ball eating fanged beast terrifyingly named Peeka. Now the drama continues as our heroine once again risks her life battling yet another frightening creature! Okay, it was a seagull, but if you think that you don't ever deal with dangerous nature living in the city, listen to this.

One morning last week while I was trying to explain to the cats that they could just WAIT for their breakfast because 'Mummy' needs a LOT more 'beauty sleep' these days, there was a sudden clatter out on our deck. Now, we are 15 floors up, so I figured either Santa and his reindeer had arrived a few months early or the window cleaners had fallen to their deaths and in either case, I'm thinking I've got a HUGE mess to clean up. However, it was neither of those. It turns out one of the lesser lights of our local seagull community had fallen onto our deck, and couldn't get up! When this bird was going to J. L. Seagull elementary, he obviously skipped out of *Glassed-In Patio Training 101*. He insisted on trying to fly away through the glass panels that surround the deck, which was, in a word, physically impossible. So he's COMPLETELY freaked out. Do you know how a freaked out seagull deals with this kind of situation? He vomits and poops…everywhere! I can sort of understand this behaviour, I was exactly the same on my wedding day.

So now my husband and I are trying to show him how to FLY off the deck, we're flapping our arms like idiots, but I had a sneaking suspicion he wasn't paying attention. I'll tell you, when you're trying to wrangle a four foot wingspan and a beak that can eviscerate a Macdonald's French Fry with one lightening peck, you're reluctant to get too close.

But I felt strongly that we had to return this proud creature to the beautiful concrete wilderness that he came from, so I grabbed a big beach towel, (I figured since gulls spend a lot of time at the beach, he'd find that soothing) threw it over him, took hold of his body, and as I lifted him up, he poked his beak out. I thought he was about to gouge out my intestines, but instead, our eyes met, beast and human, and I said "You're free little bird. You're free!" I let him go and with one beat of his powerful wings, he rose up, took one lingering glance at me, as if to say "Thank you human friend", and then he dropped a massive torpedo on the windshield of my car. That's gratitude for ya.

The Travel Bug

Coffee, Tea or Valium?

I have come to hate flying. I long for a better way to get from point A to point B, like 'beaming', as in *Star Trek*. Oh, to simply step up on to a transporter platform, nod my head to the operator, and Shazzam! My molecules are blasted apart and fired across the ocean where 3 seconds later they're re-assembled in a delightful farmhouse somewhere in Tuscany, ready to start my holiday fresh as a steaming pannini.

Of course, just like on *Star Trek*, sometimes the transporter might malfunction, and your molecules could be improperly re-assembled when you beam down, leaving you with an arm sticking out of your rear end. I would happily live with my arm there, if it meant I could avoid a 10 hour flight.

I have two big problems with flying. First, you are jammed into a large cigar tube. Second, you are jammed into this cigar tube with other PEOPLE! I was on a long flight once with a man a few rows back, who coughed every five seconds. And when he coughed, he dug right down to his ankles and let rip from there. After two hours of this, I finally had to say something, "Excuse me sir. I was wondering, is this your LUNG? Because it just landed on my bag of nuts!"

Then there are people who must speak AS LOUD AS POSSIBLE so that everyone, including the flight deck, can enjoy their BRILLIANT conversations. I was on a flight last week and there was a woman behind me who talked at maximum volume from the moment she sat down until, well, she NEVER stopped! It's like she was mainlining rocket powered caffeine. Let me give you a smattering of what she said, "….and if I push this button the seat comes up are you going to have something to drink I was thinking about ordering a beer but then I remembered it's 7 AM Ha Ha Ha Ha I brought this gossip rag look at Paris Hilton can you BELIEVE her have you heard Nick Lachey's new song it is SOOO pathetic you know when I breath in my nose gets cold once I ate an entire bag of licorice and the next day my whole body was covered in a seeping rash on average everybody loses 80 hairs a day but I think I lose 62 is that a walrus…" And it went on and on. I'm not normally a violent or suicidal person, but I was praying that the plane would fly into the side of a mountain, just to make it STOP! So somebody PLEASE get that beam thing working, because if I have any more flights like this, my arm won't be attached to my butt, but it'll definitely be INSERTED in somebody else's!

So-Cal Survival Tips

A few weeks ago I decided I just couldn't take the unrelenting sunshine of Vancouver any more, so my husband and I packed up the car and drove to the unrelenting sunshine of Southern California, aka L.A., aka PDA Paradise. And so as I sit on our hotel balcony, gazing at the palm trees and listening to the soothing roar of the 405, I thought I would pass on some of my observations of Tinsel Town and environs.

First, you are not allowed to drive on Los Angeles freeways unless you have your masters in Astrophysics, due to the fact that you must be familiar with objects that move at 'Light Speed'. If you don't have the proper training, here's what happens: you're approaching the freeway via on-ramp, you pick up speed, signal to merge, check rear-view mirror, see a large yawning gap and then carefully move left, at which point you check the rear-view again only to realize with horror that a black blur is bearing down on you at somewhere close to 4 THOUSAND miles an hour (that's 650 million kilometers per pound, with the wind)! At this point you really have only two choices, scream, the way they do in those comedy movies when a carload of people are heading for a brick wall, or wet your pants, or both.

Of course the rocket ship that is about to pass you honks its horn, irate that you couldn't manage even Mach 1, but the honk is quickly lost because at that moment the vehicle is going so fast it breaks through the time-space continuum and is now in another parallel reality where Simon Cowel DOESN'T have 6 shows going simultaneously.

Then there is the state law passed recently by Conan the Republican which makes it illegal to go more than 3 days without hearing 'Diddy' mentioned in a conversation, as in "Dude, I was at a party last night with the friend of a cousin of a brother of a manager of a nephew of a sister of a friend of an acquaintance of the gardener of the mechanic of the building manager of the psychic of the urologist of the dog walker of Diddy!"

"Cool, so you KNOW Diddy?"

"Totally!"

Finally, in Hollywood if folks aren't staring at their PDAs, they're staring at everybody else's face with an intense "Hey! Are you a somebody?" look. So, I've been staring back at them with a "Yes! I'm Katie Couric!" look. No one has argued, so I think it works. Anyway, now I'm heading to a party of a friend of a half-sister of a grandmother of a step-father of a 3rd cousin removed 12 times of the person who does electrolysis on Tom Cruise. I'll get the scoop on Suri. Totally dude!

So-Cal, Not Low-Cal

Well, I'm back from my California holiday. Let me give you the highlights: My husband and I took out a small loan to pay for admission to Universal Studios. I hadn't been there since I was 13 which was many moons ago (if you're trying to do the math, I'll just tell you, yes, I'm 17). So, of course the first thing we did was hop the tram that takes you around the studio lot. It was a little disappointing. Twenty years ago this was a frightening thrill a minute trip because part way through, the tram would get attacked by Jaws. These days the shark still attacks, but he's so old he mostly just gums the tram and then starts complaining about his arthritis, and how you'd think he wouldn't *have* joint pain, considering he's made ENTIRELY of shark cartilage!

We were also disappointed because the one ride we wanted to go on, Jurassic Park, had been temporarily shut down. They said it was a technical problem, but I heard rumours that one of the Velociraptors escaped and ate 2 of the Desperate Housewives. Although they're so skinny, all of them combined would barely make one decent crudite.

One of the ways they conserve gas in Southern California is by not allowing foreigners to buy it. If you go to a self serve pump, and stick your credit card in, it will ask for a Zip Code. Being from Canada, you can't enter our kind of postal code. So I went inside to ask the fella if I could pre-pay there, with my Canadian card, something I had already done in Northern California. He explained it to me this way: NO! Well, where was I supposed to buy gas? He starts making a low groaning noise, like an elk or gas station clerk in terrible pain, but offers no answer. However, he'll rest easy, knowing he foiled yet another attempt by an alien to GIVE THEM MONEY!

As you know, California is a leader in reducing pollution and developing alternative fuels. One of the alternative fuels that they are using more and more is Natural Gas and they get their supply of natural gas from people that eat in the restaurants there. Go into just about any restaurant and order say, a grilled cheese sandwich, and a plate will be delivered to you that is piled with enough food to feed ALL of Saskatchewan.* And when you look around you, you see the place is filled with people who are HALF the size of Saskatchewan. Each one a walking bio-fuel gold mine. I was in one restaurant in North Hollywood that had a breakfast PASTA on the menu. Pasta with eggs! I just couldn't do that. I decided to go for the mile high stack of pumpkin pancakes instead. Don't ever say *I'm* not an environmentalist.

*Province in Canada best known for its flatness, being the birthplace of Universal Health Care, and for having the world's most prized collection of dung beetles.

Really Helpful Travel Info

I was in Boston a few weeks ago for some sightseeing. First, some pertinent historical facts about Boston:

- One of the most famous events in American history happened in Boston in 1773. As a protest against taxes on tea by the English crown, crates of the stuff were dumped into the harbour, which became known as The Boston Tea Party. What is not so well known, is that to celebrate their defiance, everyone was given a slice of Boston cream pie, but because they had no tea to wash it down with, 14 people choked to death on the dry cake.

- All of Canada's Boston Terriers are shipped directly from Boston. That was a major demand by the U.S. when Brian Mulroney was negotiating NAFTA. The Americans wanted guarantees that they could export their Boston Terriers without terrier tariffs, and Mulroney demanded that in return we be allowed to export Howie Mandel to the States. So, pretty good deal for us.

One of the things you learn very quickly about Boston, if you are driving into the city for the first time, is that there is not ONE road that runs straight, without branching off at some point to become another road. Plus, you can't find a street sign anywhere! We had a map, but that just became something we could tear apart with our teeth when we were screaming with frustration.

We were so lost at one point, that we just stopped the car and called the hotel to get directions. My husband gave the cross streets, said we could see Fenway Park, home of the Red Sox. And the fellow replied helpfully, "I have no idea where you are. Just go toward the tall buildings." The gas station guy pointed us down a road, but neglected to mention that this road, like every other road FORKS OFF without warning! And we, of course, would invariably be in the lane that was forking the completely opposite way we wanted to FORK! I was ready to call the mayor at 10:30 at night and tell HIM to FORK OFF, with his crazy streets!

Suddenly it dawned on me; they'd done this on purpose. You see, the Revolutionary War got its start in Boston, and after beating the British, they vowed that no one would ever be able to attack Boston again. And believe me, there is no way an invading army could sneak up on that city. They'd be stopping at every other 7-11 to get directions, and probably Big Gulps for everyone, because they'd be tired already from all the FORKING OFF. So by the seventh or eighth 7-11, somebody would probably call the authorities.

This might be a lesson for cities everywhere. Because really, who needs Homeland Security when you can just FORK OFF!

Please Stow Your Knockers

They were running a security test at Toronto airport when I was leaving last week. I believe the test was: Let's see how long we can make thousands of people stand in the security check lines before someone takes their plastic souvenir CN Tower, and starts indiscriminately shoving it up people's back passages while screaming "Can you see the observation deck yet?!"

Believe me, I understand the need for security. I want to be as safe as the next guy, as long as the next guy isn't Evil Knievel. Everything was coming off for this check, shoes, hats. They made my husband unbuckle his belt. I wanted to yell "One moment madam, that's my job!" But they might just translate that as "I have a nuclear warhead hidden in my pants!" and suddenly I'm off to that all-inclusive Guantanamo Bay Resort. When my stuff finally went through the x-ray machine, my carry-on was pulled aside, but I wasn't worried because, as per instructions, my tweezers, my small scissors, essentially all tools dealing with unwanted hair were safely tucked away in my suitcase.

"May I look in your bag ma'am?"

"Can't think of anything I'd enjoy more!" (No Cuba for ME)

At this point, a small man whose job, apparently, was to stand and witness the slow moving lines, came over and asked the security woman who it was who had instructed her to pull my bag aside. I believe he did this because my line had been picking up speed, and that wasn't allowed. Once he'd slowed the line down to a pace a snail would find a little sluggish he backed away, proud of a job well done. And that's when she found it.

"Is this your knocker ma'am?"

Oh oh. I had put a brass knocker I'd bought in my carry-on without thinking. It's shaped like a happy sun, with pointy brass sunbeams radiating from its glowing face. It sort of looks like one of those weapons that Ninja warriors use, although it would have to be a Sumo/Ninja combo, because it weighs so much. Okay, I'll confess. This was my cunning plan. I'd sneak my knocker on the plane, and then I would quietly attach it to the locked cockpit door. And then I'd knock.

"Say Gerry, is that someone knocking on the locked cockpit door?"

"I think so, but you know the rules Tim, no one gets in."

"But it sounded like a ***door knocker*** shaped like a happy sun!"

"Oh, well in that case."

And that's when I would enter the cockpit and demand to be flown to any country that doesn't have Ben Mulroney.* I've come to really dislike flying. We'll talk more about that later, but right now I have a souvenir CN Tower that needs extracting.

Please Return Your Seat to the Upright Position...No Charge

Remember the good old days of air travel, when the flying was easy and your nuts were free? I can actually recall a time so far back, when everybody wore their best clothes when they flew. That was in case we had to make an emergency landing on a remote tropical island on the day when they were crowning their new king, and therefore we'd all be dressed for the occasion.

Sadly, those days are gone and I'll admit that I'm not happy with what's replaced them. As you know, Air Canada* is now charging for food and blankets and pillows. Mark my words, this is where it's heading:

CAPTAIN: Morning folks, Captain speaking. Sorry about the turbulence. We do have clearance to climb to a higher elevation to smooth things out and I'm happy to do that for just 5 dollars per person. We'd appreciate exact change, however we can make change for an extra 5 dollars. Thank you, enjoy your flight.

Here's another travel trend that makes me a bit nervous. For some time now in the UK, people have been purchasing flights on certain airlines for one pound. Roughly 2 dollars Canadian.

Of course, that's one way. For the round trip, it costs a whopping 4 dollars Canadian. I read the other day that you can get a return flight to Prague** from the UK for 7 dollars Canadian. That's right! Prague. 7 dollars!

So, I have some questions. Number one: at 7 dollars, what do you fill the fuel tanks with? Positive thoughts? "I think we'll fly, I think we'll fly, I know we'll fly, I know we'll...hey, why did it suddenly go so quiet?!" Number two: You're on your $7.00 round trip flight to Prague, and you ask the flight attendant for the sixth time for that cup of coffee you paid 5 dollars for, and he turns and says "Hey! What do I LOOK like, a flight attendant?" So, what's your comeback? "I beg your pardon! I'll have you know I paid 7 DOLLARS for this flight!!"

Now the person sitting next to you is outraged, "You paid 7 dollars? I paid $9.50!! What a rip off! I coulda used that 2.50 for a round trip to MARS!"

So once you land you decide to complain to the Captain about the terrible service until you discover that the plane was being flown by a woodchuck, because that's all a 7 dollar round trip will get you. But at least it explains the rough landing and the strange clumps of fur all over the plane. Oh well, who can fight this?

So next week I'm heading to Tibet on Bozo Air for 79cents return. The owners are a bunch of clowns, but at least the whoopee cushions are free.

*Official slogan "You've tried the rest...now try the one that's always in a bad mood!"

**Pronounced Πραγυε

Off To My Grape Reward

I needed a few days off last week to get away from the hustle and bustle, but mostly to try to wipe memories of Larry King's "Hey! I'm The First One with a Hurricane Katrina Special!" special from my brain. The great thing about Larry is that he can always get the world's leading experts on his show. That's why Celine Dion* was there. She knows a lot about disasters and water, because once, one of her push-up water bras burst. When Charles and Camilla got married Larry had leading royal historian Joan Rivers on, who detailed Camilla's dental work without ever being able to blink.

Anyway, that's why I headed for the beautiful Okanagan for some golf and wine tasting. If you haven't been there, and even if you have, there are a number of interesting facts about the area that you might not be aware of, which I am happy to pass on to you now.

1) Okanagan is an old Indian word that means "Land where prairie folk go to retire."

2) The actual Okanagan was created back in the '70's when then premier Bill Bennet** wanted a designated area where he could send people who say things like "Ooooo, nice nose, nice legs, not

too presumptuous" or "You'll taste chocolate, cherry and just a hint of grass on a dewy October morning", and they wouldn't be laughed at.

3) Thousands of people are moving to the Okanagan to escape the fast paced life of the big city. They want time to smell the roses, contemplate life. And then they get in their cars and blast around country roads at 3 thousand kph***. However, there are thousands of 'Traffic Calming' devices all over the Okanagan. They're called deer.

4) There's a very gregarious bird there called the Clark's Nutcracker. They chatter all the time. They're also prevalent in Alberta. The Clark's Nutcracker got its name after former prime minister Joe Clark**** married Maureen McTeer.

5) The vintners LOVE to quote ratings from The Wine Spectator magazine. "Oh, this Chateau Malamute got a 99.9998!" Whenever I see the magazine in people's homes, it's usually in the bathroom. So how important can it be?

6) When you play golf, at every hole there is always a large group of California Quail who laugh at flubbed shots, which means they laugh at ALL of mine. Interestingly, there is a lot of quail on the menus in restaurants in the Okanagan.

Well I have to leave it there because Larry King's on again. He's talking to that world famous levee expert Don MacLean*****. And meteorologist Pamela Anderson is giving tips on how to prevent frizzies during a flood. I think I need another holiday already.

---

*Canadian singer who was born in Quebec(which is located next to Spain) who hits incredibly high notes by repeatedly pounding herself on the chest.

**A premier in Canada is like a governor in the U.S. In this case, he was the premier of British Columbia, which is located next to Spain.

***This is the metric measurement for speed, kilometers per hour. Converted to miles per hour, it would equal 14 Imperial pounds, with the wind.

****Nobody outside Canada remembers prime minister Joe Clark…actually, nobody inside Canada remembers him either.

*****Of course, this was when Hurricane Katrina swamped New Orleans, and folks there were left to sink or swim by the President's emergency preparedness team, which was later re-named "The Bush League."

Big Words, Bags and Bam!

I thought this week I would write about the new Gateway Transportation Plan for the Lower Mainland.* I figured I'd say something illuminating by using big words like, "initiatives" and "sustainability". Plus I would make witty commuting statements like, "Our transportation arteries are so plugged, we're suffering from *ARTERIAL SCHLEROSIS*!"   Ha, Ha! And then I remembered, Hey, I'm not that smart!

Then I decided to write about the biggest tragedy of the week: The Paris Hermes store wouldn't let Oprah buy a trillion dollar handbag. Hermes says they were closed. Oprah says Hermes is racist. I have to say, I think Oprah has misread this one. She believes that the Parisian staff rudely refused her service because she's black. Oprah, come on! Parisians don't care what colour you are. They're rude to *EVERYBODY!*

Anyway, in the end I decided to write about a new study conducted by scientists (who obviously graduated in the bottom percentile) that have discovered how to tell if a woman is faking an orgasm. (Now, I realize that the word orgasm may be disturbing for some people, so when you see "orgasm" just think "origami") I knew right away this had to be a study conducted by men. They've been suspicious for years. From cave man days:

GRUG: Ugh, good for you?

GRUGETTE: Ugh, yeh, yeh sure…look a mastodon!

To present day:

GEORGE: Ugh, was it good for you?

GEORGETTE: Yeh, you're the best…look it's Regis Philbin!

So men have been desperately searching for a tool that will tell them we're faking, and they finally found it. No it's not *When Harry Met Sally*. It's a Positron Emission Tomography machine. That's right; they scanned women's brains while having an orgasm and while faking an orgasm and guess what? When we're faking an orgasm, nothing shows up on the brain scan. Isn't science wonderful! Just imagine, stuck inside one of these big machines, with doctors watching you from behind the glass:

DR. BOB: Okay, we're showing her a picture of Alex Trebeck naked. Anything?

DR. ED: Nothing.

DR. BOB: Now we're showing her a picture of a trillion dollar Hermes handbag.

DR. ED: Holy 4th of July, stand back, she's gonna blow!!

I know where this is going. They'll start selling home versions of these brain scanning machines to guys so they can finally catch us. So if you're on a date and he invites you back to his place to see his "big Positron machine", just tell him you forgot that you had to get home early. You've got some origami to catch up on… by yourself.

---

*A billion dollars to widen bridges & freeways so that we have a lot more people to look at when we're stuck in traffic.

Season's Bleatings

Cupid, Kilts & Pressurized Water

A few thoughts for Valentine's Day. First, if you are in need of a gift for the special man in your life, I have something that is guaranteed to make your guy's pupils dilate, his heart rate quicken and his body vibrate with unbridled excitement: a pressure washer! Oh, believe me, once they get that magic wand in their hands and feel the power that sprays forth, they are never the same.

Several years ago when we were living in a house, my husband bought one to clean the concrete after a long, dark, wet winter, and from the first blast of water he was addicted. He power washed everything, the cars, the windows, the cats (who weren't entirely appreciative) I didn't see him for days. Then women from the neighbourhood started knocking on the door, "Hi, can Bob come over…with his powerful nozzle? My gutters are filthy!"

We're in an apartment building now, so we got rid of the pressure washer, but a while back we had a young fellow here blasting the lichen off the concrete walls. My husband took an instant dislike to him. He said he swaggered. Of COURSE he swaggered. He had a power washer!

If you're in need of something for the lady in your life, I read last year about male window cleaners who wear kilts. They don't say what they wear UNDER the kilts, but apparently they do come with their own squeegee. Here's a Valentine's gift I don't recommend. I heard a commercial on the radio the other day for a supplement for men that will, um, extend their amorous performance to such a degree that people will notice the difference in the man, especially at work. Well, call me crazy, but I think that instead of listening to some guy go on about how many hours he added to his love making, co-workers would be much more interested in hearing how he found a new route to work and took hours OFF his commute. Finally, the biggest love story of the year, the NASA astronaut charged with assaulting her romantic rival. She wore a diaper so she wouldn't have to stop as she drove all the way from Texas to Florida. My man, being the romantic he is, wanted to know where you could buy a car that gets that kind of mileage? The good news is, NASA has just announced that she has been chosen for the first manned mission to Uranus...although maybe that's where all the trouble started in the first place.

The bad news is, I believe this could become the new trend in judging if a guy is dating material. Remember Seinfeld? Pretty soon women will only go out with a guy if he's "diaper worthy!" Well...if he wears a kilt and has a pressure washer, pass me the Huggies.

Like a Steak Through My Chard

I like meat. I mean meat in the sense of nutrition and sustenance, not in *The Days of Our Lives* soap opera sense, where the guys with the 36 pack abs strangely always manage to have their shirts blown off at the beginning of every episode…um, maybe I am talking about meat in that sense too, but that's for another time.

So when I stumbled upon a blurb in the paper promoting a feminist/vegetarian-philosopher(*what the…?*) giving a talk about patriarchal values and meat-eating I was very curious, and once I'd looked up 'patriarchal' in the dictionary, well, I felt a tad guilty. I thought, yes, I probably should go and hear about how women have been oppressed down through the ages by fathers wielding giant cuts of inside round. I'm sure the feminist/ vegetarian whatsit has some valid points and I should just get off my rump roast and support the sisterhood. But you know, after cleaning three bathrooms and trying to raise two cats to be responsible citizens who contribute to society, I'm just *too* tired. And anyway, I pretty much got the drift in those few lines, "meat-BAD, anything with a sprout-GOOD". However, there was a time when that's exactly how *I* thought. Many years ago, I decided to stop eating anything that had a mother and I convinced my not-yet husband to do the same…and he married me anyway! Believe me, when you go vegetarian, your friends and family very quickly come to hate you. When you get a dinner invite, the most common thing you hear is, "I just didn't know what to make for you guys, so I got you some nice pencils to chew."

This leads me to my greatest dinner disaster. One Christmas I came across Tofurkey, a turkey replacement made with tofu. I bought a box complete with fake turkey, fake stuffing, fake gravy and fake gas (which was remarkably life like). I thought, fantastic! Who'll ever guess we're not eating the real thing and we'll be saving a life in the process. But for some reason the 'glob' just never seemed to cook, so after about 18 hours I removed it from the oven, and let me tell you, when you bring something to the table that resembles a pod that an alien baby is about to erupt from, nobody says, "Oooo, yummy!"

Well, due to the fact that everyone who was at that Christmas dinner is still in therapy, and also because I simply ran out of mouth watering recipes for groats, we are back to eating flesh. And I'll be honest, I would never go back. Although, there are days when I do get a hankering for a nice juicy HB pencil.

Mi Casa Es Su Casa...Now Get Out

Well, we have a new government. Oh, I'm thrilled. No really. I haven't been this excited since maxi-pads got wings. But if they're going to remain the government for any length of time, then they need to bring forward bills in the house that all the parties will vote for. And I have the perfect one. I recommend they pass a bill making it illegal for any visitors (friends or family) to stay in an individual's home for more than 48 hours. I believe there would be absolutely no opposition to this bill. I speak from experience.

Over the Christmas holidays we had relatives from 'The Old Country' staying with us for a month. Thirty days! THREE-OH! Here's the funny thing. I love getting the guest rooms ready. I wash all the sheets, fluff all the pillows, put flowers in vases, get fancy soaps, shampoos, bubble bath, embroider their names on towels, write personalized songs to sing when they arrive, it goes on and on. And I can't wait to get them from the airport and show them their cozy rooms.

VISITORS: This is so cozy…is that a man standing in the corner?

ME: Yes, that's Bjorn, he's your own personal masseur that I hired just for you while you're visiting!

VISITORS: Wow! We are going to LOVE staying with you!

ME: And it's only a month, what a shame.

And then something happens, usually somewhere between the eighteenth and thirty-seventh hour that they are with us. I'll be sitting at the kitchen table chatting amiably with our guests, when all of a sudden I'll hear this evil demon voice in my head, and it's screaming "Who ARE you people and WHAT ARE YOU DOING IN MY HOUSE!!!"

I feel terrible, but it's uncontrollable. I'm about to sit down and watch TV but the GUEST has the remote! Again the demonic Exorcist voice in my head, "Excuse ME! That's MY remote, can you not read my name on it…TO-SHI-BA!?"

In less than two days I've gone from wanting to give my guests the full 'Martha' experience, to wanting to beat them to death with a small appliance. We could downsize, but I know that wouldn't help:

VISITORS: Hey, Linda, we're coming to visit for 9 months!

ME: That WOULD be FABULOUS! But unfortunately we've moved into a large hairy man's armpit, and we just don't have the room.

VISITORS: Oh…rats…well, is his OTHER armpit free?

ME: Well…yes…but…

VISITORS: FANTASTIC! We'll be there tomorrow!

Anyway, our visitors are gone now. Of course I mean gone home, not 'gone to meet their maker' due to an unfortunate and mysterious curling iron incident. So get that bill passed prime minister. If you don't, well, next time you're in Vancouver, why don't you come and stay at my place for a few days.

All the Tidbits Fit to Print

As a 'serious journalist' I have a number of responsibilities that I take, well, seriously. That's how you become a 'serious journalist'. When I went for my job interview to be a 'serious journalist', the first question they asked me was, "Are you SERIOUS?!" And I replied, "Hey! Are you kidding? I'm WAY serious...seriously!"

So, one of those serious responsibilities is to supply you with enough mind blowing tidbits to make you the hands down most entertaining person at your next party. I didn't have this kind of responsibility in my last job. I used to be a road construction flag person. The money was a lot better, but I felt my expression was severely restricted, because it seemed to me there just had to be SOMETHING in between Slow and Stop. Mosey? Tootle? Sashay? I don't know.

Anyway, Fantastic Piece of **Party Tidbit #1**- Liza Minnelli has announced that she is SICK OF SEX and would not want to live with anyone ever again. This news came as a great relief to thousands of gay and straight New York men over the age of 60.

Party Tidbit #2- Talking about his new boss this week, David Emerson*, Minister Responsible for Dodging Protestors, made the comment that prime minister Harper** is a "Hard Ass." Well, that's the ONLY part of his body that's hard.

Party Tidbit #3- Authorities in Tennessee have been trying to catch a black bear that attacked humans, so in an effort to trap it, they placed doughnuts in a cage. So far they haven't caught the bear; however they have trapped 7 police officers.

Party Tidbit #4 – The Queen celebrated her 80th birthday this past week. When asked how she was going to mark such a special occasion, she said as usual she would spend it with the one who has been by her side for so many years. They would go for a quiet walk, have dinner together while they watched CSI: Miami, and then just before bed she would give him a kiss and a tickle on his rump. A reporter said that it was wonderful to know that after all these years, she and Phillip still had such a warm relationship. "GOOD GOD! I'm not talking about Phillip! I'm talking about Dickie my favourite Corgi!"

Party Tidbit #5- A man was arrested in the states for pretending to be a doctor and going door to door offering FREE breast exams to women. They finally caught him after one woman became suspicious because…he wasn't using gloves. As a public service, here is a tip that will help spot anyone fraudulently offering up breast exams, prostate exams, etc.: If it's a doctor making a HOUSECALL, it's definitely a scam.

My work is done. PARTY ON PEOPLE!

---

*Cabinet minister who started out as a Liberal and the day after his party got hammered in a federal election, contracted a rare virus known as OhcrapIminthewrongpartycoccalus.

**Canada's current leader, who never met a G8 buffet he didn't like.

Peace On Earth & Other Christmas Legends

Today, beautiful Christmas traditions. In Austria, they not only have St. Nicholas, but they are also visited by someone called Krampus. Krampus is supposed to scare away evil spirits and so has a face that looks like something out of a Wes Craven movie. This year some folks in Austria wanted to ban Krampus because they say he scares kindergarten children. But it's actually the adults who are terrified of him, because with all his fangs and clawed hands, he reminds them too much of tax auditors.

This lovely story got me thinking about another Christmas tale you might not be so familiar with although it reverberates throughout this holiday season. This one comes from England, specifically the town where my family sprang from, Little-Corned-Beef-On-Rye near Piddling Upon Chutney, Corningware County. Way back in the Dark Ages, things were very dark. It was dark during the day and even darker at night. This went on and on for, well, ages, and people became very bored. So the town decided to put on a celebration to break the monotony and they chose the end of December, the coldest time of the year, when it's most difficult to visit and shop, mainly because they were NUTS!

Anyway, the night before the big celebration, one of the town elders, a roly-poly man with a long white beard had been enjoying quite a few horns of fermented Tripe juice. When he staggered back to his wattle and daub hut, his key wouldn't work in the door. He thought his wife had locked him out again, so he climbed up onto the roof and started to slide down the chimney. But, he was at the wrong hut, and the residents thought someone was trying to steal their collection of dirt, so they set their guard goat on him and just as his legs were hanging down in the fireplace, the goat grabbed his pants and yanked them right off!

The old man fell to the floor screaming and then raced out of the hut, through the village and off into the woods and wasn't seen again, until the following December when he rode back through the village on December 24th, wearing no pants, in a sleigh pulled by eight goats. As he passed by the villagers, he would yell out "Where are my #!@* pants?!" And then he would moon everyone.

And that's how St. Nickersless was born. Many people feel that in these consumer driven times the true meaning of St. Nickersless has been lost. I disagree. I think St. Nickersless is alive and well and can be found at many office parties this time of year, especially if there's a Xerox machine handy. May the spirit of St. Nickersless live on in you this Christmas season.

And Goodwill to All...Except the Crappy Pianist

I have PTPSD. Post Traumatic Party Stress Disorder. Okay, let me back up just a bit. We had our big Christmas party last weekend. Family and friends "donning their gay apparel" and wassailing, which I believe is still legal in most provinces. In general I think the party was a success, primarily because there were no fist fights. (Memories of a family wedding in England, but that's another story)

However, there was one moment of severe embarrassment for yours truly. Knowing me as you do, you're probably saying to yourself "Linda, surely severe embarrassment is as familiar to you as looks of incomprehension are to Stephane Dion*" and you'd be correct. You see, I had promised to play the piano for the singing of Christmas carols. Now, most everything I play has a dirge-like quality to it. Plus I use a 'Search and Destroy' method when it comes to hitting the right notes, but I thought if I practiced I'd at least be able to hammer out 3 easy carols.

I began with *Deck the Halls.* On the first try I managed to get all the way to "Deck the halls with..." when I lost my bearings

141

and started playing something that you might hear in a really disturbing nightmare. So I started again.

On my second attempt I didn't quite make it through the first "Deck" when I fell apart! The crowd was getting restless, desperately wanting to move beyond the first word of the song and I could sense if I didn't find at least one note that sounded familiar I'd soon be pelted with mince tarts and cranberry sauce. So in order to save the buffet, I had to stop playing. Luckily we had an emergency room doctor in the group who had 'good hands' on the piano as well, and even though he was Jewish, he didn't mind getting us through *Joy to the World*.

But I was pretty embarrassed because, well mostly because I stunk the joint out. And I know in the future if I ever proclaim, modestly, "I'm not really very good at the piano," instead of being reassuringly supportive, folks will just say "Oh you're not just whistling Dixie, sister!" I realized that playing the piano is like testifying at the Gomery** Inquiry…it's all about the fingering.

There is something good that has come from the pain. I've decided to hire myself out as a piano player, but not for the usual weddings and bar mitzvahs. I think there's a market for a talent like me to play at divorces and funerals for people that nobody liked. And then when someone says,

"Geez, that pianist at Horrible Harry's funeral was TERRIBLE!"

The response will be "Yeh, but somehow it suited him."

And the great thing is, I won't need to practice.

*Former leader of The Liberal Party of Canada. French is his mother tongue. Unfortunately English was his ugly stepsister tongue, which became the main reason for the 'former' above.

**Hard to believe, but politicians were investigated for corruption. I know, you're feeling faint from the shock. Fingers were pointed, some folks were sent to jail, and once again our children are safe.

LaVergne, TN USA
21 November 2010
205756LV00001B/97/P